THE HUGHIE GALLACHER STORY

THE
HUGHIE
GALLACHER
STORY

PAUL JOANNOU

BREEDON BOOKS
PUBLISHING COMPANY

First published in Great Britain by
The Breedon Books Publishing Company Limited
45 Friar Gate, Derby DE1 1DA
1989

ISBN 0 907969 58 5

Printed by The Alden Press Limited, Osney Mead, Oxford.
Jacket designed by Graham Hales Artwork and printed by Arkle Print,
Round Spinney, Northampton.

CONTENTS

Introduction

FOOTBALL, for me, is about characters and personalities. The game would never be the huge attraction it is, but for those highly-talented players who perform the extraordinary, are flamboyant and at times controversial. In one word, they entertain, be it on or off the field.

Hughie Gallacher fits all those categories and more. Perhaps no other footballer, before or since, had such a remarkable career. From the working-class heartland of industrial Lanarkshire he became the idol of thousands. His life was one of sensation, glory and tragedy, a fascinating tale.

Married at 17, he tragically lost his first son, was separated by the time he was 20, and almost died from pneumonia before joining Airdrie in 1921. A Scottish Cup victory and three successive Championship runners-up positions followed as well as the Scots' centre-forward shirt. He became a national hero north of the border and much wanted by big clubs in England. Newcastle United tried and tried for his signature, at last succeeding in a record deal, and he went on to skipper the Geordies to the Football League title in 1927. Goals came in regular abundance, in twos, threes, fours and even fives. So

did trouble with referees, fellow players and officialdom, his temper being on an ever-lit short fuse.

Chelsea paid another record amount in 1930 and he strode around the capital like a London toff. But the south also brought him problems, appearances in court and bankruptcy. A second marriage followed and a move to the Midlands. He almost won another Championship medal with Derby County, then had spells at Notts County and Grimsby Town and returned to Tyneside with Gateshead.

He played until he was 36, spanning 20 seasons of football and scoring over 400 goals in 624 appearances, and all with a diminutive 5ft 5in stocky build. One of the immortal Wembley Wizards, he was a regular for Scotland, netting 24 goals in only 20 games. He was a folk hero to home fans, a villain to many others. Then came a tragic ending in 1957, when he committed suicide as he was due to appear in Gateshead Magistrates' Court. Yet his personal tragedy can never dim great years of triumph on the football pitch. Years after his death the name of Hughie Gallacher is still known, even to youngsters who were born well after his sad demise. His is a compelling story, one I've enjoyed writing immensely.

Paul Joannou
Edinburgh
July 1989

Acknowledgements

APPRECIATION is noted to several people who have helped in various ways in fitting together the life story of Hughie Gallacher. A special thank you to Hughie's eldest son, Hughie junior, who since the point of contact in 1988 has been as enthusiastic as the author in seeing this book come to fruition. Family mementoes and memories have been included in the text, without which the book would have been largely a 'paste-and-scissors' exercise.

Airdrieonians' historian John Henderson supplied a wealth of information, as did his Queen of the South counterpart in Dumfries, Bill Hume. The following people have also been a great help:

Ann Anderson (Newcastle), G.Bradley (Rochdale), 'Dally' Duncan (Brighton), John Diamond (Hebburn), Scott Cheshire (London), J.W.Errington (Newcastle), R.Fyfe (Wallsend), Walter Lawrence (Newcastle), George & Alice Mathison (Gateshead), Nicola Rippon (Derby), Joan Smith (Blackpool), Les Triggs (Grimsby), Andy Ward (Oxford), Sid Woodhead (Grimsby), W.H.Swann (Cheshire), A.Wilson (Tyne & Wear Museums Service). The Association of Football Statisticians is also acknowledged.

Editor Graeme Stanton and journalist Paul Tully of the *Newcastle Evening Chronicle* are thanked for permission to use the vast library in Thomson House. The staff of the Central Library, Newcastle-upon-Tyne, have been ever helpful as were the National Library of Scotland and Bellshill Library, especially Catriona Wales.

Photographic Credits

P.Joannou Collection, *Newcastle Chronicle & Journal,* Hughie Gallacher junior, John Henderson, Walter Lawrence, Bellshill Library, Ian Cormack.

Foreword by Tommy Lawton

I WAS only 15 years old when I first saw Hughie Gallacher play. It was at Ewood Park, Blackburn, just before Christmas 1934, and the home supporters were really getting on his back, calling him 'useless' and a 'waste of money'. Hughie was playing for Derby County that day and he answered those Blackburn fans in the only way he knew — by scoring five goals. Derby won 5-2 and Hughie Gallacher maintained his reputation as one of the greatest centre-forwards ever.

After the match I was introduced to him and he ruffled my hair and told me: "Young man, keep your nose clean and you'll do all right in this game." Poor old Hughie, of course, knew all about that. He'd had a fairly traumatic time off the field and in many ways he was a rather misunderstood man, certainly nowhere near as black as people liked to paint him.

Happily, all the stories and rumours about him never overshadowed his immense talent. He was a truly great centre-forward — and when you consider that Hughie was only about 5ft 5in tall, then what he achieved was staggering. He had remarkable ball-control and he was brilliant off the ball, reading the game perfectly and always knowing where to go. I think he must have had springs in his heels because, despite his small stature, he could outjump the biggest centre-halves of the day. Of course, he took a terrific amount of physical punishment, but he never shirked a challenge. If he was around today, then I don't think £2 million would buy him. Players like Hughie Gallacher appear only once in a generation.

Tommy Lawton

CHAPTER ONE

THE TANNA 'BA' PLAYER

"To be paid for playing soccer! I just could not believe it."

Hughie Gallacher

'MATHA' Gallacher was a striking character, a stocky farm worker from the north of Ireland with the sort of prominent, tailed moustache that was common in those Edwardian days. The likeable Protestant arrived in Lanarkshire, if not to find his fame and fortune, then to eke out a modest living in industrial Scotland at the turn of the century. He was one of many to make that trek from the Emerald Isle.

He found employment in the Lanark coalfield, down the pit at Bellshill. Matthew met and married a local girl, Margaret, who was also a staunch Protestant. Both became active members of the local Orange Lodge.

It was one of the couple's sons, Hughie, that did find fame and, by comparison, a bit of fortune too. But that was quite a way off. Matthew and Margaret had two sons. Hughie was the youngest; the first-born was John. The family settled in Lanarkshire, one of the most highly industrialized and densely populated counties in Scotland. The Industrial Revolution had transformed the area. Those were days of iron and steel masters, coal barons and shipyard

empires of the Clyde. Coal-mines went further and further into the surrounding Lanark hills and contrasts were extreme. From a dour landscape of pit-heads, steel-works and towering slag heaps, to gently rolling Scottish countryside of pleasant fields and glen.

Hughie Kilpatrick Gallacher was born in the early hours of 2 February 1903. Queen Victoria had died less than two years before and Edward VII was on the throne. The Prime Minister of the day was a Tory, Arthur Balfour. It was still an upstairs-downstairs Britain — the rich and the poor, with little inbetween.

Gallacher was born into the town of Bellshill, today a community almost swamped by the Glasgow sprawl and surrounded by motorways that carry traffic quickly past without a stop. Ten miles from Glasgow and five miles from Hamilton, at the turn of the century Bellshill relied on heavy industry: coal, steel and the local railway works. At its peak the town had as many as 20 pits, while at Mossend — one of the four attached villages forming the community — the Neilson Ironworks was one of the biggest in Britain.

In Edwardian Lanarkshire, society was experiencing a relatively prosperous time. Work was available and men with families, like the Gallachers, arrived from far and wide. Bellshill's population was cosmopolitan and numbered 15,000 or so. Like 'Matha' Gallacher, many were of Irish upbringing, both Protestant and Catholic, in those days before the partition of Ireland in 1921. The *Lanark County History* records that harmony between the religious groups was not good. 'Unfortunately there is little fellowship between Roman Catholics and Protestants', the official report noted. Besides the Irish, there were a number of Lithuanians and Poles. They all came to work in Bellshill's collieries and ironworks.

Bellshill was not what you would call a health spa. It was tough, rugged and functional — one main street with rows of terraced houses running off at right angles. It was fortunate to be on the main Edinburgh to Glasgow road and possessed all the requirements of a working-class town. It even had a notorious photographic studio run by an Englishman, Harry Teece. Inside his small premises he held wild parties with a number of prominent young ladies. The chief relaxation appeared to be photographing the women in all manner of nude poses.

Bellshill was also famed for its profusion of pubs and an official report commented that there were 'far too many'. There was a prevalence of betting, gambling and drinking, often as a refuge from the pit or steelworks. To the young Hughie Gallacher this was the norm and perhaps, in later life, it was one reason why he found it difficult when criticized for his own 'off the field' activities. Bellshill produced men who were down to earth, rough and tough, and Gallacher could be counted in that breed.

The Gallacher family was a close body. Hughie was particularly attached to his mother — he rarely made a single move throughout his playing career without discussion — yet she continually gave him a scolding as a kid, for kicking out the toes from his shoes and boots. Bellshill loved its football. On every street corner or piece of waste ground, boys would kick anything that moved — stones, cans, even a bundle of rags tied together with string — for they rarely had a real football. At most they could afford a small rubber ball that cost a few pennies. Hughie Gallacher was one of those street laddies and his parents found it difficult, if not impossible, to make him take an interest in anything other than soccer.

Hughie said about his introduction to football: "I started biffing a twopenny ball on the school playground." It was an origin not uncommon for Scottish footballers. That elusive rubber sphere and school playground were the starting points for many a Scots star to be — and the ' Tanna' ba' player ' evolved and became a well-used expression north of the border.

Bellshill can boast several famous footballers. Apart from Gallacher, Alex James was born in Mossend, Sir Matt Busby hails a mile from Bellshill Cross, while two more Scottish internationals, John Gilmour, capped with Dundee, and John Plenderleith, of Manchester City fame, were born in the town.

Hughie's father and mother in later years, pictured with son John and his wife Jeanne.

Much more recently, Rangers star Ally McCoist comes from the area. It was former Manchester United boss Busby who said of the people of Bellshill: "The inhabitants were interested in having babies and looking after their menfolk if they were females; coal-mining and football if they were male."

The Gallacher brothers attended Bellshill Academy and it was there that Hughie became seriously involved with football. At the age

11

THE ACADEMY AND WAR MEMORIAL, BELLSHILL.

of ten he won his first medal, thanks to the misfortune of his brother. John Gallacher was due to play in goal for the school side in the Rose Bowl Final, a competition in which all schools in the district took part. Unfortunately for John, he was sent on an errand by his mother and broke a leg when he tripped on his skipping rope — he skipped everywhere. Up stepped Hughie to don the goalkeeper's jersey. He was only a wee chap, but his school won the game 2-1 and Hughie saved a penalty to cap a marvellous display. That was his first medal and, thereafter, Hughie was a regular in the school side, in various positions

(opposite): Bellshill Academy. Hughie and John attended the school, as did Alex James.

from goalkeeper to outside-left. At that tender age, he dreamed of becoming a star goalkeeper. Before he left Bellshill, Hughie captained the school team and appeared for Lanark County.

It was at Bellshill Academy that Gallacher became very friendly with a school pal and, like himself, a football star in the making — Alex James. In his biography of James, the writer John Harding records him as saying: "Hugh and I hit it off right from the start. We scrapped together and dogged together (played truant) and we romped the streets together . . . the two of us would do anything for a game." Hughie reinforced those comments, saying: "We used to kick anything we could lay our hands on." The two 'tiny tots', both to end up a mere 5ft 5in at most, got up to all sorts of tricks to play and watch the game they lived for. James said: "The snag was finding the ball. They were as scarce as gold to us. So we used to spend three ha'pence for a sheet of paper with verse printed on it and then go round from door to door

(opposite): Bellshill Cross, the centre of town just before World War One.

A group of Edwardian Bellshill miners pose after a stint in the Lanark coalfield.

trying to collect pennies." They would collect enough and buy a tanna' ba', which would keep them going until the next window was broken and the ball taken from them, a frequent occurrence. Gallacher and James played and played, practising for hours on end.

The two friends also watched football whenever they could afford it. They were brought up on the great Celtic side of the 1900s and they adored 'Nap' McMenemy, Jimmy Young and Patsy Gallacher in particular. Religious barriers meant nothing to the young Protestants and at Parkhead, both hero-worshipped Patsy Gallacher. He was a 'mighty midget' too; Gallacher admitted later that he received many

Celtic in 1914. Gallacher watched them whenever he could. Back row (left to right): W.Maley (manager), McMaster, Dodds, Shaw, McNair, Johnstone, McColl, Quin (trainer). Front: McAtee, Gallacher, Young, McMenemy, Browning.

13

lessons by watching his namesake in the green and white hooped shirt.

Patsy Gallacher. Hughie's namesake and idol as a child.

World War One came and killed and maimed many. During those years Gallacher was barely into his teens and he worked in munitions factories at Mossend. By the time the Treaty of Versailles was signed in 1919, he was down the pit, like virtually everyone else — and if it wasn't the colliery, then it was the steelworks. Gallacher was toughened in the coal-mines. Long hours at the coal-face and perspiration from manual work held him in good stead for the future. He could never have sustained the punishment he was to receive on the football field, had it not been for his hard upbringing.

Another facet of his childhood that went some way to affecting his footballing career was his love for boxing. Two of his school chums became professional boxers and British champions, featherweight Johnny Brown and welterweight Tommy Milligan, who later became European champion at middleweight. Hughie always fancied himself as a boxer. He sparred regularly and trained at a locally renowned gym in Hamilton, used by his friends. He was never afraid of the bigger man, was aggressive and short-tempered and could throw quite a punch. He certainly had the right background for the pugnacious game he was to play.

Normality slowly returned after war, but with it came economic

Boxers Johnny Brown (top) and Tommy Milligan. Both sparred with Gallacher before he turned to professional football.

depression and no district in Scotland suffered more than Bellshill and the surrounding area. Elsewhere the depression and financial crisis did not really start until 1929, but Lanarkshire felt its effects throughout the inter-war period. From 1920, steelworks closed and coal-mines were sealed up. Long

years of unemployment and its attendant problems touched almost every home and social life was dramatically affected. The rows of inadequate housing deteriorated, some to turn to slums, and the once fairly well-off became increasingly poor. Hughie Gallacher had a chance to get out — football was his escape.

Gallacher and James continued their footballing progress together by playing Scottish Junior football, a strange misnomer. 'Junior' football in Scotland is, in fact, played by all ages, youths and adults. Lanarkshire was a strong area then, with several noted clubs. Surrounding Bellshill were Orbiston Celtic, Crusaders, Douglas Hawthorn, Holytown Thistle and Bellshill Athletic. The two pals offered their services to several teams, including Bellshill Athletic, one of the most powerful sides which, in 1919, lifted the Lanarkshire Junior Cup, a prestigious trophy in Scotland. Bellshill officials were not impressed, though. They just laughed at the two tots. 'Far too small', was their answer. The youngsters did, however, get to push the club's hamper to and from the station for away fixtures and earned half a crown for their troubles.

Gallacher rarely let his size or build deter him from aiming for the top and competing with 6ft tall, 13st contemporaries. At 5ft 5in and never more than 10½st, he never let it affect his game. The laws of the game were not designed for little 'uns, but both he and James overcame the difficulties.

Despite being the youngest, Gallacher was the first of the two budding footballers to climb the ladder to fame. James was almost 18 months older but throughout his career, especially in the early years, he saw Gallacher overshadow him. Hughie signed for Tannochside Athletic when he was 16, playing as an amateur in the Lanarkshire Juvenile League. In a mining community two miles from Bellshill, he settled at centre-forward and soon grabbed four goals in one match. Gallacher moved to another mining team, Hattonrigg Thistle, very close to his home, and began to create an impression.

Gallacher's first real break came early in 1920. He often watched Bellshill Athletic, on this occasion against St Mirren Juniors, and by chance they were a man short. Officials recognized him in the crowd and asked him to fill in. Naturally, Hughie jumped at the opportunity. He ran out in front of almost 5,000 fans, a huge ordeal for a youngster. Nevertheless Gallacher acquitted himself well, netting in a 1-1 draw – a lucky break that turned into a decisive move. He soon signed for Athletic, the club that had laughed at both Gallacher and James a couple of years earlier.

His joy at joining such a noted club was overshadowed by something of a family feud. Gallacher had two uncles who helped run neighbouring Larkhall Thistle, another respected club. They also wanted to sign the up-and-coming youngster. But Hughie wanted to play for his home-town side and chose Bellshill. He was promised a signing-on fee of £10. It never materialized, perhaps an omen of the ill-luck that was to follow him around in the future.

Gallacher was on his way. His pal Alex James, by comparison, was still struggling to find a top Junior club, but soon he would follow Gallacher — and into League soccer

Alex James, during the 1930s, in his days with Arsenal.

too. James signed for Raith Rovers in 1922 and later starred with Preston and Arsenal, winning Cup and Championship medals as well as eight Scotland caps. The paths of James and Gallacher crossed many times in the coming years and, on more than one occasion, Hughie would plead with his club management to sign James. Newcastle United officials told Gallacher that they thought James was too small. The Geordies did not move for him and lost his services to Arsenal.

With Bellshill Athletic, Hughie Gallacher created a huge reputation. He regularly found the net, possessing a formidable shot in either foot. His twists and turns, feints and wiles confounded defenders, while he was able to spring up for a cross and mostly had the edge on the much taller centre-half when the ball was crossed. His strong point, though, was his remarkable ball control, his quickness off the mark giving him the edge on his marker. The rough edges had to be removed, but the sign of a genius was there to see.

Willie Bell, who was for many years secretary of Athletic, recorded that, in his view, Gallacher's best game for any club, including his professional days, was for Bellshill against Vale of Clyde at the Tollcross ground. Hughie was carried off three times, returned three times and put the ball in the net three times. It sounds dramatic, but true or not, is one man's memory of a player who was soon to become a massive idol.

Before Gallacher made the next step in his footballing career, the first of many controversial incidents during his life occurred. In July 1920, at barely 17 years of age, he was married to Annie McIlvaney, a Bellshill girl he met at the coal-pit he worked in Hattonrigg. She was from a Catholic family and this, on top of such a young age to marry — a rare occurrence then — caused family relations to be strained for a while. They had no home of their own, staying in rooms and later with parents. It soon became clear that both Hughie and his wife were far

Gallacher, the 'junior' player in his late teens, soon to sample senior football.

too immature to take such a step. They stayed together for only a year and, tragically, their son died before he was 12 months old. They separated, but a while later decided to try and live together again. They had another child but separated permanently in July 1923, when Hughie Gallacher was 20. Ramifications of that marriage were to stay with Hughie for over a decade.

On the football field, Gallacher found happier days. His reputation was growing. In December 1920 he was picked for the Scotland Junior side to play Ireland on Clyde's ground at Shawfield Park. He was 17 years old and grabbed the equalizer in a 1-1 draw, a header from ten yards out and with only two minutes left to play. Hughie was ecstatic. There was a double celebration, for it was on his brother John's wedding day too. Hughie dashed away after the game to be best man.

Only a matter of days after that big occasion, Queen of the South acted quickly to secure the signature of Hughie Gallacher. The Bellshill lad was elated: "It was heaven with all the trimmings. To be paid for playing soccer! I just could not believe it." The Scot was well on his way to becoming a star. Not as he had dreamt, as a goalkeeper, but as a centre-forward.

CHAPTER TWO

CUP TRIUMPH

"Defenders don't get much time for thinking when Hughie's about."

Daily Record

JAMES Jolley was the man who was particularly impressed with Hughie Gallacher's performance in that Scotland Junior international. He was secretary of Queen of the South, then a relatively new club, founded in 1919 and not yet in the Scottish League. They played in the Southern Counties Cup and local competitions but, most important, played against Reserve or 'A' sides of the big Scottish League outfits. It was one step from first-class soccer.

Jolley nobbled Gallacher straight after the international. Subject to a trial game, he offered him a signing-on fee of £30 and £5 per week plus all travelling expenses from Glasgow to Dumfries. Gallacher was more than a little surprised at the quickness with which Jolley moved for his signature. However, Hughie was more than pleased to sign for the Palmerston Park club. He said: "I had to travel on a Friday and return home on a Monday or Tuesday. That seemed good to me. Five pounds, even after the war years, was better than a shift down the pit for a meagre wage."

On 29 January 1921, Hughie Gallacher ran out in the blue and white of Queen of the South for a friendly against St Cuthbert's Wanderers. It was a runaway 7-0 victory, helped by the visitors arriving without a goalkeeper, a local player standing in. Almost 1,500 were present and saw this line-up:

Woods; Murray, Coupland, Christie, Ballantyne, Connell, Gray, Aitken, Gallacher, Dallas, Stillen.

Gallacher passed his trial with ease. He netted four goals and the local paper, *The Standard,* noted: 'Gallacher created a favourable impression. A young player of dashing type'. His next game was Hughie's first in senior football, against Nithsdale Wanderers in the second round of the Scottish Cup. A big crowd of 5,000 saw Queens go down 3-1. Again he impressed: 'Gallacher, who was the best of the line, played well throughout'.

For the rest of his short stay on the Solway coast, Gallacher found goals easy to come by. He registered 18 in his first seven games. Some of the opposition proved inadequate to say the least and Gallacher remarked: "Playing for Queen of the South was money for nothing." Against Dumbarton 'A' he had an outstanding game against a defence including experienced League men. Queen of the South won 5-2, Gallacher netting all five goals, and Press comments were flattering: 'The Palmerston wizard had matters all his own way and his lightning methods when out for goals, shooting with deadly accuracy with either foot, or butting in with his head as opportunity offered, won him additional favour amongst the Palmerston supporters'. After the game he heard that a senior club had watched him. That club turned out to be Airdrieonians.

Hughie again netted four in one game — this time Glasgow Railway Select were on the receiving end — and yet four more against a strong Queen's Park Hampden XI, the reserve combination of the Scottish Division One side. Gallacher could not stop scoring in this level of football. Then, in April 1921, he grabbed a wonderful goal against the team that had already watched him, Airdrie.

Queen's went down 3-1 to the Lanarkshire clubs reserves, but Gallacher's goal was a gem and must have impressed the watching officials. *The Standard* recorded the moment: 'A long pass from Gallacher to Gray let the winger off and, beating Watson, he carried the ball practically to the goal-line. A beautiful centre from the winger found Gallacher with his back to goal, but with a wonderful overhead kick he screwed the ball past Fotheringham into the net'. It was typical Gallacher. He would always score tap-in goals, but could also net the spectacular effort with regular ease.

His last game for Queen of the South was a week later, on 13 April 1921 against Royal Albert, and he signed off with a goal. In less than four months, Gallacher had sent 19 goals into the net in only nine games. His reputation was growing rapidly. Queen's had little hope of keeping his services. Rules in those days allowed a player not in League football to be a free agent. Several scouts had made the trek to Dumfries and once on his way back to Glasgow, Hughie was captured by Johnny Cochrane, then St Mirren boss and later in charge of Sunderland. Cochrane spent all of the two-hour journey trying to coax Gallacher to sign for the Paisley club. Hughie said he would think about it and contact him, but before that could happen, the young Scot was rushed to hospital with double pneumonia and that gave Airdrie the chance to step in before St Mirren could react.

It was only a matter of days after the game against Royal Albert that Hughie was in hospital, seriously ill. He was placed on the danger-list for a few days at Dumfries Infirmary and his parents were summoned from Bellshill. He was laid up for five weeks. Doctors said, after he had recovered, that they thought he would never play football again. Gallacher made the comment: "It seemed my brief tilt at fame was finished."

It was when Hughie was convalescing in Bellshill that Airdrie FC decided to make their move for the 'titch' of a man with a hunger for goals. The Scottish League club had watched Hughie several times. Gallacher recalled the first meeting when he was still with Bellshill Athletic: "I went with a pal of mine to see a game in which Wishaw were engaged on their own ground. As we stood watching the match, the centre-forward of the home team lost a reasonable chance. My friend said, 'You would have found the net there Hughie'. Two yards from us was standing John Weir, a very astute Lanarkshire colliery contractor, who has had a finger in the pie in scores of big football deals." Weir was associated with Airdrieonians and contact was made. It proved an important meeting. Not only did Weir prove invaluable in getting Gallacher to Broomfield

Park, home of Airdrie, he later became a Newcastle United scout too.

It was Airdrie manager, John Chapman, together with a club director, who called on Hughie Gallacher at his home. Hughie recalled: "It was not a happy-looking day I can assure you. It was raining heavily. I was reading a newspaper when my mother announced that some gentlemen wanted to have a chat with me." Gallacher was taken by complete surprise, but was not going to let the chance of Scottish League football pass him by. He slipped on a jacket and donned a waterproof and was sped away to Broomfield Park, or so he thought. He ended up at an undertaker's office near Airdrie Cross, the business of one of the club's directors. The terms suited Hughie and he signed the forms, surrounded by wreaths, coffins and other mournful paraphernalia. He joined Airdrie on 9 May 1921.

Gallacher had turned 18 years of age and now earned £9 per week in the season and £6 per week during the summer, with a 10s (50p) bonus for a draw and £1 for a win. The working lad now had a chance. In those days the Scottish footballer was a folk hero. If he made it, no matter how small, he filled the role of the aristocrat of the working

(opposite): Hughie in Airdrie colours just after signing from Queen of the South.
Airdrie's squad in 1921-22. The young Hughie Gallacher is in the centre of the middle row. Back row (left to right): Thom, Drinnan, Price, Dickson, Walker. Middle: Murdoch, Dick, Cornoch, Henderson, Gallacher, O'Hagan, Malcolm, Taylor, Allan, Ellis, Preston. Front: McQueen, Bennie, Hart, Russell, Reid, McCulloch, Doyle, Bradley, Knox.

class. As it turned out, Gallacher found much success in the years to follow, but he also found it difficult to cope with stardom.

Airdrieonians were a mediocre Division One side, the Scottish League then consisting of 22 clubs. They were never spectacular and never threatened the Rangers-Celtic domination of domestic football. However, in the coming years, the men with the red diamond on their white shirts were to change that. They gradually built a team to challenge the Glasgow 'Old Firm' and Gallacher was an important cog, grabbing a century of goals for the Waysiders.

Hughie did not make the first team immediately and had to serve virtually a two-year apprenticeship. Manager John Chapman soon moved on, to Manchester United, and in his place came the former Scotland and Celtic half-back, Willie Orr. The 1921-2 season was a poor one for Airdrie. At one stage they were third from bottom of the League, but the nucleus of a famous side was slowly coming together. The centre-forward shirt was held by several players: Willie Henderson, who netted 36 goals in the previous season; Jimmy Reid, an influential player in the following months; and a handful of youngsters, including Gallacher.

Hughie made his Scottish League debut against Raith Rovers, a holiday weekend match on 19 September 1921. Airdrie lost 2-0 at Broomfield Park. The side was:

Shortt; Dick, McQueen, Neil, Knox, Hart, Reid, Bennie, Gallacher, Dickson, Thom.

Hughie Gallacher was left out for the next game, but in the Reserves he scored profusely, snatching hat-tricks with ease — threes against Celtic, Hearts and Motherwell and five goals against Hibernian. The Reserves also did well in the Second XI Cup, defeating Albion Rovers in the Final. Local Press reports were commending, but some had reservations: 'Gallacher has many excellent points as a centre and he may yet find his place there. Pity he hadn't a few more inches stature'.

Airdrie goalkeeper Shortt and full-back Dick, both in the line-up against Raith Rovers in 1921, Gallacher's first in senior football.

Hughie netted his first goal in League football against Clydebank during November and at the turn of the year was given a run in the side. In January 1922, against St Mirren, Airdrie won 4-1 and Gallacher made his mark, claiming a hat-trick, the first of many in senior football. Airdrie climbed away from the bottom of the table and although Hughie missed more chances than he scored, the crowd

and media reaction was good: 'Despite many failures at goal, Airdrie folk appear to have a relish for Gallacher as a trier and one who gets among the opposing defence'. Hughie netted seven goals in 15 matches in his first season. It was a satisfying start.

The following season, 1922-3, saw Airdrie's fortunes change dramatically. They finished runners-up to champions Rangers and a formidable team full of exciting skills had taken shape. Gallacher was included in the opening show against Hamilton and got the winning goal, but for the early months of the season he was in and out of the line-up. Boss Willie Orr even signed two new centre-forwards and Gallacher thought he would never be given the extended run he so much wanted. In the Reserves he again scored goals by the bagful, as well as being part of the team that won the Scottish Alliance championship. It was only a matter of time, though, before he would claim that leader's shirt for his own. When the chance came he grabbed it and appeared in 20 games all told that year. No one took the first-team shirt from him again.

The Diamonds, with Gallacher in the side, reinforced their position as second club to Rangers. Against Motherwell during March, Hughie gave a brilliant demonstration and scored three in a 4-1 victory. His third was a cheeky strike. 'Athlete' noted, 'That goal was a natty affair, for when the centre trapped the right winger's centre he threw the opposition off the scent by back-heeling the ball into the net and so created his hat-trick'.

Airdrie's forward line had been given rave reports. They possessed speed, playing ability and a unique understanding. Jimmy Reid was the commanding veteran and was with Airdrie for most of his career as a striker. He was the general and, now at outside-right, had a great understanding with Gallacher, able to drop centres at the far post for the centre-forward to capitalize on. Willie Russell was a dainty schemer at inside-right, a beautiful player to watch. He eventually left to join

Jimmy Reid, an influential player in Airdrie's side.

Preston for a big fee, money which paid for a new stand at Broomfield. At outside-left was Jimmy Somerville, able to get goals, and into the side for the new season came a young forward named Bob McPhail. Only 18 years old, he and Gallacher were the youthful scoring sensations and McPhail later won 17 international caps and honours galore for Rangers. Only Jimmy McGrory netted more goals in Scotland than McPhail's 300 plus.

Other members of the Diamonds' fine side were Jock Ewart, a Scottish international goalkeeper who had been south with Preston, and centre-half Jackie McDougall, a whole-hearted player who also appeared for Scotland, and another who left Broomfield in a large transfer deal, this time to Sunderland. Bob Bennie possessed admirable skills at left-half, yet another to be honoured by his country, and transferred for an inflated sum.

For 46 years Airdrieonians had been striving to win one of Scotland's two major prizes — the Championship or Scottish Cup. In 1923-4, at long last, that moment arrived. In the League it was a repeat performance from the previous year, finishing runners-up to Rangers again. Highlights included a 6-1 win over Clyde early into the season, a game that saw Gallacher net five

goals to put Airdrie top of the League. Wingers Somerville and Reid supplied the ball with automatic precision and Hughie's finish was deadly. All five goals were practically unstoppable and it was a wonder that he didn't equal Bob McColl's then record of six goals in a match. *The Daily Record* noted: 'Gallacher is a virile centre who knows his place and gets off his mark in double-quick time. Defenders don't get much time for thinking when Hughie is about'.

SCOTTISH DIVISION 1						1922-23
1 Rangers	38	23	9	6	67:29	55
2 Airdrie	38	20	10	8	58:38	50
3 Celtic	38	19	8	11	52:39	46
4 Falkirk	38	14	17	7	44:32	45
5 Aberdeen	38	15	12	11	46:34	42
6 St Mirren	38	15	12	11	54:44	42
7 Dundee	38	17	7	14	51:45	41
8 Hibernian	38	17	7	14	45:40	41
9 Raith	38	13	13	12	31:43	39
10 Ayr	38	13	12	13	43:44	38
11 Partick	38	14	9	15	51:48	37
12 Hearts	38	11	15	12	51:50	37
13 Motherwell	38	13	10	15	59:60	36
14 Morton	38	12	11	15	44:47	35
15 Kilmarnock	38	14	7	17	57:66	35
16 Clyde	38	12	9	17	36:44	33
17 Third Lanark	38	11	8	19	40:59	30
18 Hamilton	38	11	7	20	43:59	29
19 Albion	38	8	10	20	38:64	26
20 Alloa	38	6	11	21	27:52	23

How Airdrie finished seasons 1922-23 and 1923-24, both as runners-up to Rangers.

SCOTTISH DIVISION 1						1923-24
1 Rangers	38	25	9	4	72:22	59
2 Airdrie	38	20	10	8	72:46	50
3 Celtic	38	17	12	9	56:33	46
4 Raith	38	18	7	13	56:38	43
5 Dundee	38	15	13	10	70:57	43
6 St Mirren	38	15	12	11	53:45	42
7 Hibernian	38	15	11	12	66:52	41
8 Partick	38	15	9	14	58:55	39
9 Hearts	38	14	10	14	61:50	38
10 Motherwell	38	15	7	16	58:63	37
11 Morton	38	16	5	17	48:54	37
12 Hamilton	38	15	6	17	52:57	36
13 Aberdeen	38	13	10	15	37:41	36
14 Ayr	38	12	10	16	38:60	34
15 Falkirk	38	13	6	19	46:53	32
16 Kilmarnock	38	12	8	18	48:65	32
17 Queen's Park	38	11	9	18	43:60	31
18 Third Lanark	38	11	8	19	54:78	30
19 Clyde	38	10	9	19	40:70	29
20 Clydebank	38	10	5	23	42:71	25

It was in the Scottish Cup that Airdrie found success with an extraordinary run to the Final. Hardly a tie escaped controversy. In the first round the Lanark club met Morton and were a goal down with barely ten minutes left. They grabbed a dramatic equalizer and then, in the final 60 seconds, Gallacher hurled himself at a cross, missed it, and in doing so distracted the Morton 'keeper to allow Willie Russell in for a last-gasp winner. There were claims that Gallacher, who ended up in the netting with

the ball, was offside, but the goal stood. St Johnstone proved no problem in the second round. Airdrie coasted through, 4-0 victors, and in the next tie Motherwell were thrashed 5-0 with five glorious headers, two by Gallacher and two by Russell included. Airdrie were now many people's Cup favourites.

The quarter-final proved a much more difficult obstacle. It took the Broomfield club four matches and almost seven hours of football to rid themselves of Ayr United. The first meeting ended 1-1, Gallacher snatching a late equalizer with a speciality overhead kick. Four days later a scoreless draw resulted at Somerset Park. On neutral territory at Ibrox Park, 30,000 saw another 1-1 draw and 24 hours later, the clubs met once again at the same venue for the deciding contest. Ayr argued bitterly about refereeing before this clash — they had four goals disallowed in previous games and earned a change in officials. It was Gallacher who won the match for Airdrie, capitalizing on a goal-keeping error and netting the only goal of the replay. The Diamonds were through to the semi-final to meet Falkirk at Parkhead.

With little preparation, that crucial meeting being Airdrie's sixth match in 15 days, they faced the Bairns of Brockville. But it mattered little. Two goals by Somerville gave Gallacher's team a comfortable lead. Then, 15 minutes from the end, the centre-forward was in the midst of controversy when he was laid out prone by Falkirk's half-back William Dougal, who had given him a rough time all afternoon. Dougal was sent off, but the incident seemed to stir the Bairns into a late rally. Syd Puddefoot netted with a header and with only minutes on the clock, Jock Ewart miraculously saved a certain equalizer which earned him stitches in a wound and a hero's ovation. Airdrie, and Gallacher, were through to their first Cup Final.

Before the club's big day, Hughie Gallacher had another appointment, his first Scottish cap, against Northern Ireland on 1 March 1924. Airdrie's Cup run had flung him into the headlines. His stature broadened the more he was seen, and when Chelsea's Andy Wilson dropped out of the Scotland side, there was much talk as to who would be his replacement. Gallacher had enjoyed a marvellous season, hitting 39 goals. Dave Halliday, the League's top scorer, was also on form for Dundee, and Tom Jennings of Raith also claimed the place. But Gallacher received the nod and took his place alongside his Airdrie colleague, Jimmy Reid. The line-up read:

Harper(Hibs); Hutton(Aberdeen), Hamilton(St Mirren), Kerr(Hibs), Morris(Raith), McMullan(Partick Thistle), Reid(Airdrie), Cunningham (Rangers), Gallacher(Airdrie), Cairns (Rangers), Morton (Rangers).

Young Gallacher — he won his first Scottish cap against Ireland.

Over 30,000 saw the international at Celtic Park. Gallacher had just celebrated his 21st birthday and performed well in a 2-0 victory. Blustery winds spoiled the game as

a spectacle and it took the Scots a while to score, despite dominating affairs. Hughie had a hand in the second goal, being involved in the move that led to Dave Morris adding to Andy Cunningham's opening goal. Press comments were mixed for the young Airdrie leader. *The Daily Record* noted: 'Hugh Gallacher of Airdrie made many friends...yes, Gallacher is worthy of another trial'. But *The Glasgow Herald* held a different view: 'Gallacher has not reached international class.' Hughie still had to prove he was Scotland's next centre-forward.

The setting for the Scottish Cup Final was Ibrox Park on 19 April 1924. There were 59,219 present and the opposition was Hibernian, victors over champions Rangers and appearing in their second Final in a row, having lost to Celtic in 1923. Hibs fielded exactly the same line-up as 12 months earlier. Airdrie had a doubt in Gallacher, who had injured his ankle, but he was fit for the highlight of the season. The two teams came out of the tunnel and lined up as follows:

Airdrie: Ewart; Dick, McQueen, Preston, McDougall, Bennie, Reid, Russell, Gallacher, McPhail, Somerville.

Hibernian: Harper; McGinnigle, Dornan, Kerr, Miller, Shaw, Ritchie, Dunn, McColl, Halligan, Walker.

A week before the Final, Airdrie played Hibs in a League game and lost 2-0. That was an astonishing fixture, as Hibs, with regular goalkeeper Willie Harper on international duty and without a reserve on their books, had half-back Peter Kerr between the posts for the full 90 minutes. Airdrie were obviously in only second gear, but the Final itself was a different affair.

Hibs were never in the game. Willie Russell gave the Waysiders victory with two headers. The first was inside the opening five minutes, unchallenged from a corner. The second was just before half-time, a glancing header from a Bennie cross. The Easter Road side came

Jock Ewart who saved a certain goal in the Cup meeting with Falkirk.

closest when they had a penalty awarded and then taken away after the referee had discussed the incident with his linesman. It was Bob Bennie who dominated the game. Gallacher said: "The Airdrie lot set about the Hibs straight from the start." Even official Hibernian accounts recorded, 'And from the first minute, Airdrie had no difficulty', and 'The impression at half-time was that Airdrie had already won it'. Won it they had.

The finest line-up Airdrie has fielded, pictured with the Scottish Cup and medals. Back row (left to right): Carrol (trainer), Neil, McPhail, McDougal, Ewart, Preston, Gordon, Allan, Murdoch, W.Reid (trainer). Front: Somerville, J.Reid, Russell, Gallacher, McQueen (capt), Dick, Bennie, Howieson.

How the Evening News *saw the Hibs v Airdrie Cup Final of 1924.*

Gallacher's Scottish Cup medal.

Bob McPhail's memory in his autobiography was: "The terror-like attitude of Gallacher caused havoc with the Hibs defenders. He and Russell were easily our best forwards." Airdrie's side contained seven past or future internationals: Gallacher, Ewart, McDougall, Bennie, Reid, Russell and McPhail. It was the finest side the club has fielded.

A celebration dinner followed at Rombacks Restaurant in Hope Street, Glasgow, for Gallacher and the rest of the Airdrie party, then a journey in an open-topped vehicle through Airdrie town centre to Airdrie Cross, with the Cup held proudly aloft. Hughie Gallacher's bonus for helping to win the Scottish Cup was all of £8, not a penny more.

CHAPTER THREE

SCOTLAND'S CENTRE-FORWARD

*"No, this is a player who is not leaving Scotland . . .
and will never play for any English club."*

Airdrie director

AIRDRIEONIANS carried on from their Scottish Cup success by coming close to lifting the Championship in 1924-5. In previous years they had finished second to Rangers by a wide margin, but this campaign saw the Ibrox club beat the Diamonds by a mere three points. Airdrie were runners-up for the third successive season and were to do it again the following year, this time to Celtic.

Hughie Gallacher was on the mark again. He scored 35 goals in as many games. 'Athlete' noted: 'Gallacher doesn't make much fuss about it, but his calculating eye is always on his wings, and, my word, how he shoots'. He got off to a wonderful start to the season, scoring all three in a 3-2 victory over Kilmarnock, then grabbing four in a 6-0 win over St Johnstone a week later.

There was the story of what was, perhaps, Hughie's most spectacular goal north of the border. It came against Ayr United and also showed Gallacher's sense of humour. In a tough and close contest, Airdrie were 2-1 behind with five minutes remaining. Then Gallacher was on the spot with an equalizer — an unprecedented effort scored with a

SCOTTISH DIVISION 1						1924-25
1 Rangers	38	25	10	3	77:27	60
2 Airdrie	38	25	7	6	85:31	57
3 Hibernian	38	22	8	8	78:43	52
4 Celtic	38	18	8	12	76:43	44
5 Cowdenbeath	38	16	10	12	76:65	42
6 St Mirren	38	18	4	16	65:63	40
7 Partick	38	14	10	14	60:61	38
8 Dundee	38	14	8	16	48:55	36
9 Raith	38	14	8	16	52:60	36
10 Hearts	38	12	11	15	65:69	35
11 St Johnstone	38	12	11	15	56:71	35
12 Kilmarnock	38	12	9	17	53:64	33
13 Hamilton	38	15	3	20	50:63	33
14 Morton	38	12	9	17	46:69	33
15 Aberdeen	38	11	10	17	46:56	32
16 Falkirk	38	12	8	18	44:54	32
17 Queen's Park	38	12	8	18	50:71	32
18 Motherwell	38	10	10	18	55:64	30
19 Ayr	38	11	8	19	43:65	30
20 Third Lanark	38	11	8	19	53:84	30

Airdrie, runners-up in Division One yet again, this time in 1924-25.

spectacular bicycle-kick that made everyone gasp — the crowd, the goalkeeper and even Hughie, who said later: "Between you and me, I slipped and, as I was falling, my leg went up in the air . . .just by accident. My foot collided with the ball . . .it was the goal of the match." No stylish Brazilian would have admitted that.

Undoubtedly, Gallacher was now a feared striker and, thus, a marked man. Success and fame brought its own problems to Hughie Gallacher, problems with which the Scot could never totally come to terms. It was in 1924 that he started to receive

Airdrie in 1925. Back row (left to right): Neil, Dick, Allan, Ewart, Preston, Somerville. Front: McPhail, Russell, Gallacher, Bennie, McDougal.

regular physical treatment from defenders. Heavy challenges were commonplace and off-the-ball incidents frequent. Hughie's quick-fire temper saw him in trouble with referees, whilst the newspapers gave him a mixed Press. A meeting with Partick Thistle at Broomfield Park was representative. Gallacher scored twice in a 4-1 victory, but in a niggardly confrontation with the visitors' Irish international defender, Chatton, both players were eventually sent off for constant quarrels and brawls. They continued the row in the tunnel, with blows being exchanged. Both received stiff sentences, Gallacher being suspended by the Scottish FA for five matches, the first of several long punishments he received. One scribe of the day wrote: 'Gallacher, up to a point, was cool as an iced drink in summer. The fizzing point arrived when he was fouled, and that came more than once'.

Yet, in that game against Thistle, despite fighting with his marker, Gallacher scored another memorable goal. The newspaper account reports: 'Sometimes Gallacher is ragged for holding the ball, but after this performance never say die. Tapping and twining he lost Chatton, Crichton and Paton to finally face Ramsay and, from a bad angle, drove the ball past the goalkeeper against the inside of the far post from where it lodged in the net. Words fail to describe the incident. It was academic football lifted to a craft seldom seen. The crowd were spellbound as Hughie meandered past the varied opposition with wonderful control of self and the ball, and the cheer that finally broke cannot easily be forgotten'.

In another bodily encounter, this time a top-of-the-table clash with Rangers, Airdrie won 1-0 and inflicted Rangers' first defeat of the season. Tackles were heavy all afternoon, with Gallacher and another Irish international, this time Billy McCandless, fighting a personal duel. Incident followed incident and the Rangers man was left a passenger following one brush with the stocky Gallacher. Rangers captain, Tommy Cairns, was sent off as the match reached its boiling point, while Airdrie's Jock McDougall was carried off and winger Jimmy Somerville was knocked out. Gallacher relished that sort of atmosphere — he was never a player to hide from a tackle, trouble and a good dog-fight. He gave as good as he got, if not more, in return.

After the match, Gallacher was selected for special treatment by the Glasgow Press. *The Daily Record* reporter noted: 'I heard Rangers people and others say that Gallacher was the cause of all the trouble . . .that he should have been ordered off'. Hughie had become the subject of much talk. He was rated with the best as a goalpoacher, but controversy had begun to follow him around.

Despite his growing 'bad boy' reputation, the Scottish selectors reckoned he could well be the man they had been looking for as the country's next centre-forward. His League and Cup records were first-class, almost 70 goals in as many games. During February and March he could do little wrong and further persuaded SFA officials that he could fill the position. Gallacher made headlines whenever he appeared.

Scotland gave him his second cap on a quagmire of a pitch against the Welsh at Tynecastle, home of Heart of Midlothian, and Gallacher put on a magnificent display in Scotland's capital. He scored two goals in a 3-1 victory, the first being a fine strike, fooling the Welsh into a pass and then hammering the ball home. The second, though, was talked about for years after the event. It was another Gallacher solo effort. There were five defenders between him and the goal. With a lightning burst, he streaked upfield, the ball seemingly tied to his boot. He swerved past Keenor, then Russell stuck out a foot to block his progress. Gallacher just pushed the ball and flashed past him on his blind side. Another Welshman raced up to him. Hughie stopped

Welsh defenders Fred Keenor (right) and 'keeper Bert Gray, both beaten by Gallacher's marvellous solo effort for Scotland at Tynecastle.

dead and the defender was left utterly bemused. Only Gray, Oldham Athletic's goalkeeper, stood between Gallacher and the goal of a lifetime. Gray came out and dived frantically at the ball. He went down to Gallacher's right foot, Hughie coolly hooked the ball over the goalkeeper's body and tapped it into the net with his left boot. Later, Gallacher said: "As I turned to walk back I saw the Welsh players applauding me." Hughie rated that goal as his best ever.

He was a newspaperman's dream. There were thrills on the pitch and plenty off it too. On the eve of the international in Edinburgh a huge row blew up over an Irish reporter's allegation that Hughie Gallacher should not be allowed to play for Scotland — because, simply, he was Irish. The journalist reinforced his claim with his father's Irish background and extracts from the Irish Registry Office. A real fuss was caused until Hughie's mother rushed to Edinburgh with the original birth certificate, stamped conclusively at a parish adjoining Bellshill.

A fortnight after his show against Wales, Gallacher was in Scotland's

line-up against Northern Ireland in Belfast. He was in exquisite form again. After Davie Meiklejohn had opened the scoring for the Scots, Gallacher first hit a post, then scored and afterwards sent Jimmy Dunn of Hibs racing away for the Blues' third goal.

Following that performance, he was back at Tynecastle, selected for the Scottish 'B' side in an international trial match. He played alongside his childhood pal, Alex James, then with Raith Rovers. On that occasion, Gallacher netted five goals and a week later he got another four as Airdrie demolished Third Lanark 7-1. Three days after that he appeared for the Scottish League against the Football League at Goodison Park. Hughie scored again, along with his Broomfield colleague Willie Russell, but the Scots fell 4-3.

At 22 years old, Gallacher had established himself as Scotland's top forward and was in the side for the prestige game of the season — the meeting with England at Hampden Park on 4 April. Gallacher's rapid climb to the top caused many a rich English club to flock over the border to watch the dandy little Scot.

Scotland's side that defeated England 2-0 in 1925. Gallacher netted both goals. Back row (players only), left to right: Meiklejohn, McStay, Harper, McCloy, Russell, Gallacher. Front: McMullan, Jackson, Morris, Cairns, Morton.

Many of those scouts were in the 92,000 crowd that witnessed the home country's game against The Auld Enemy in 1925. Gallacher was again partnered by his clubmate Russell in the Scots forward line and reports were sent back to English grounds glowing with superlatives. Hughie netted both Scotland's goals in a fine 2-0 success. After 37 minutes he fired a waist-high volley which flew into the corner of the net, well out of Dick Pym's reach. In the second half, Hughie was left with only the Bolton Wanderers' goalkeeper to beat. Pym dashed out, there was a scramble and Gallacher shot into a gaping goal. Two goals in his first Scotland-England confrontation and 11 goals in five international appearances in the season was a remarkable achievement, and more was to follow.

The renown that Gallacher had created in that 1924-5 campaign was phenomenal. But, despite his obvious footballing talents, he was a difficult individual at times, more so for the opposition, but also for his teammates. In his biography, *Legend*, Bob McPhail noted: "He was a selfish wee fellow, he thought of no one but himself . . .he had a vicious

Bob McPhail, pictured in Scotland's jersey later into his career.

tongue and he used it on opponents. I learned swear words from Hughie I had never heard before." Yet

McPhail acknowledges he was a winner on the field: "A superb centre-forward, and he knew it . . .he had a superb sense of getting himself into the right position . . .he was never caught off balance. He shielded the ball probably better than any other player I've seen."

Gallacher began the new season with intense transfer speculation in the air. Scores of rumours started to circulate regarding a proposed transfer to one of the glamour English clubs. The reality was that Airdrie's success brought scouts to their doorstep virtually every other week. One by one, most of their stars departed for big fees to top outfits. Russell went to Preston, McDougall to Sunderland, Bennie to Hearts and McPhail to Rangers. Gallacher had the choice of several clubs but Airdrie would not let him go. They constantly denied approaches and put up the 'not for sale' notice. The official comment was: 'No, this is a player who is not

Three of Gallacher's colleagues. Bob Bennie, Jock McDougall and Willie Russell.

leaving Scotland . . .and will never play for any English club'. They told Hughie to ignore the paper talk and concentrate on his football.

That was difficult for the Bellshill lad to do, but all the conjecture did not affect his game. He followed on from the previous year by knocking in goals from all angles and at the highest level, too. Playing for the Scottish League at Cliftonville, Belfast, in November 1925, he destroyed the Irish once more by netting five of Scotland's goals in a 7-3 victory. It was a Scottish record and only two other players, Barney Battles and Bobby Flavell, have scored five in a senior international fixture. Remarkably, all of Hughie's goals were in succession and three inside 14 minutes. That achievement placed Gallacher into more controversy, though, and almost cost him his life.

At half-time a note was passed to the dressing-room from Irish partisans saying that Gallacher would be shot if he did not ease up and stop scoring. Hughie, of course, ignored the threat. The extremist home fans were not to be taken lightly. Before the Scottish party sailed for the mainland, Hughie ventured to visit friends in the city. He was warned to be careful, for then, as now, Belfast was no place for strangers. The little Scot just grinned — until a bullet splattered on a nearby wall as he walked near Queen's Bridge. Whether it was a real attempt on his life or a grim practical joke will never be known. Gallacher could see the funny side afterwards: "I'll have to extend my stay in Belfast. It seems I still haven't managed to teach the Irish how to shoot straight." But Gallacher was shocked at the incident, and he recalled much later: "If ever a world record was set up for the 100 yards, I did it then. I never showed myself out until it was time to move homewards."

Back in Scotland, transfer speculation continued to fill the back pages and it angered loyal Airdrie fans. Gallacher was regarded almost as a god at Broomfield Park. He could do no wrong. At one stage the Press had him signed, sealed and

delivered to Notts County, with Hughie knowing nothing of it. Fans were in uproar, showing their disapproval at anyone connected with the club. Even manager Willie Orr's wife was insulted, caught by a group of supporters on her way to church. Gallacher was besieged at his home in Bellshill. He recalled: "I had to lock the door and pretend I was not at home." The Notts County deal was pure newspaper speculation but it was inevitable that Gallacher would depart, despite Airdrie's insistence he would stay.

The large demonstrations, the threats — even to burn down the Broomfield grandstand — could do nothing to stop his eventual departure. Gallacher's skills were in prime demand; he was fast, elusive and difficult to knock off the ball. Close to goal, he was sharp and able to take chances with either foot, or with his head. He was slick in the short pass and brilliant at making chances for others. He was a top crowd-puller. Sunderland wanted him and so did Newcastle United. Everton were linked with his name, as were two of London's big sides, Arsenal and Chelsea, plus a handful of lesser clubs.

It was Newcastle United who persisted, though. Sent packing by Airdrie directors on several occasions, they would not take no for an answer. Gallacher's last match for Airdrie was on 5 December 1925, a 2-1 defeat at the hands of Morton, and by coincidence an historic reverse. The Waysiders' fabulous home run of 67 League and Cup games without defeat came to an end. It was over three years since a visiting team won at Broomfield Park. Hughie had netted exactly 100 goals for Airdrie in only 129 appearances. The following Tuesday, Hughie Gallacher was a Newcastle United player, at the start of a fabulous decade in the English First Division.

Gallacher — subject of much transfer speculation.

27

CHAPTER FOUR

TYNESIDE'S HERO

"As I ran out the deafening cheers turned to a . . .
oh! The crowd had just noticed how small I was."
Hughie Gallacher

LONG-SERVING Newcastle United secretary, Frank Watt, said of the Gallacher transfer saga: "It took weeks, aye months of parleying, repeated conflabs, almost innumerable rebutts and the most painfully fluctuating negotiations before we pulled off the deal." Many times Newcastle were represented at Airdrie fixtures and everyone knew it. On the first occasion directors Bob McKenzie and John Graham trekked north, they witnessed Gallacher net two beauties. Hughie said: "It was impossible to tell how many times they watched me. It would be idle for me to tell you that I was unaware of their presence." Gallacher was very ambitious and although he loved Airdrie, wanted a big move. He never pushed for it, but never hinted that he would reject an offer if and when it came.

Newcastle United became very determined. They had sold their Scottish international centre-forward, the ageing Neil Harris, and urgently needed a replacement. On a visit in November 1925 they saw Airdrie's master goalpoacher have a superb game and the Geordies decided there and then that they would get their man, whatever the cost, no matter how ridiculous the transfer fee. The following Tuesday, United's party travelled north to ambush the Airdrie midweek board meeting. Secretary Watt and directors Graham and McKenzie turned up at Broomfield Park to a frosty reception. Airdrie boss Willie Orr said confidently to Watt: "Take it from me that my people will never transfer Gallacher." Hard cash, however, demolishes even the strongest of principles; every man has his price and Gallacher was no exception. Eventually, United's team was granted an interview with the Airdrie board. The Tyneside trio spoke bluntly and gave little time for the Airdrie men to get a word in. Their tactics were simply to persuade the Airdrie men to name a figure. They asked: "Finally, what'll you take?" An Airdrie director fell for it and named a sum of 'about £6,000'. Naming the amount was all the Newcastle contingent wanted. They jumped in and offered more. Airdrie's officials, shocked at the figure, agreed.

Dejected boss Willie Orr was despatched to fetch Gallacher from his home in Greengairs, not far from Airdrie. It was a cold, wet and wild evening. An astonished Gallacher was in his pyjamas and hardly noticed the rain blowing over him. He dressed and followed Orr back to Broomfield to meet the Newcastle United officials. Hughie did not take much persuasion to cross the border. He related: "England had always seemed to offer the greatest opportunities and though I was only a lad, I soon decided to accept the move." At a late hour on Tuesday, 8 December 1925, a telephone message was received by the remainder of United's eagerly waiting board back on Tyneside. Gallacher had agreed terms and a new record fee had been established.

That fee was the subject of much speculation. A week before, Sunderland paid £6,550 for Bob Kelly, to create a new record. On the news of the Gallacher deal, wild rumours spread. £10,000 was mentioned. The *Newcastle Daily Chronicle* noted: 'Seven thousand pounds is generally the accepted sum', but the fee was never released. The club's official comment was: 'The sum paid is the club's business and theirs alone'. In record books to date the fee is recorded as £6,500. This looks on the low side and it appears that Kelly's record of £6,550 was beaten.

Tyneside's Press heralded Gallacher's arrival as the coup of the decade. United were congratulated on signing 'the most famous centre of the day'. They reaped praise in every newspaper. 'Newcastle United Football Club has effected the smartest stroke of football business that has been transacted in modern times,' said one report. The 22-year-old from Bellshill joined a more than competent Newcastle squad. The Magpies won the FA Cup in 1924

Frank Watt, Newcastle United's long serving secretary. He led United's negotiations with Airdrie.

and had finished high in Division One every season since the war. The club wanted the League Championship and Gallacher was going to fill the missing link that would bring the trophy back to Tyneside. He was

Gallacher, pictured shortly after joining the Magpies.

a vital acquisition and everyone had confidence that the Scot would succeed in English football.

Gallacher arrived in Newcastle on Friday of that week. United journalist, pen-named 'Hereward', remarked on his arrival in the city: 'A quiet spoken pleasant young fellow'. Another said Gallacher possessed a 'boyish appearance'. It was the start of 14 seasons in English soccer — a period of much glory and many sensations, or, as Gallacher put it: "I was branded a trouble-maker, stormy petrel, problem player — these were just a few of the lesser things said of me." He became the most talked-about player in the game and, despite all the controversy, scored over 300 goals in the coming years.

Gallacher's debut in the Football League was a Division One encounter at St James' Park between United and Everton on 12 December. Both sides were in midtable and what turned out to an 'exhibition game' ended 3-3. St James' Park bubbled over with expectation before the kick-off. As the players came out, Newcastle fans had their first view of Gallacher, the player who was to become a Geordie hero like no other since. Hughie said: "The home fans cheered the first few players tremendously. As I ran out the deafening cheers turned to a . . .oh! The crowd had just noticed how small I was. Never had I been more aware of my size." He hardly looked like a footballer that was to take the Magpies to honours.

The teams for that day were:

United: Wilson; Hampson, Hudspeth, McKenzie, Spencer, Gibson, Urwin, Cowan, Gallacher, McDonald, Seymour.
Everton: Hardy; Raitt, McDonald, Peacock, Reid, Virr, Chedgzoy, Irvine, Dean, O'Donnell, Troup.

Tyneside's initial disappointment was quickly dispelled. Gallacher immediately got into his stride, netting two goals and laying on United's other for Stan Seymour. Centre-half Charlie Spencer recalled: "Gallacher had a big name in Scotland but we were staggered

Stan Seymour. Later known as 'Mr Newcastle', on the score-sheet in Gallacher's debut match against Everton.

Charlie Spencer soon knew that his club had secured a star. Later, as manager, he signed Gallacher for Grimsby Town.

by his size. Then, soon after the match began, I turned and gave my fellow defenders a thumbs-up signal. We knew a real star had joined us." Gallacher's first goal in English football came on the half-hour. Willie Gibson sent the ball to the edge of the penalty-area. Gallacher had his back to goal, took the pass, pivoted, chased between the Everton backs and swept the ball past the advancing goalkeeper. It was a classic.

United should have won with ease, but after establishing a 3-1

lead, their defensive mistakes allowed the Merseysiders to make a comeback. All three Everton goals came from young England centre-forward Dixie Dean, a man who was to be Gallacher's great contemporary over the next decade. The

Dixie Dean in action. He was Gallacher's great contemporary and netted a hat-trick on Hughie's first appearance for United.

Newcastle Evening Chronicle enjoyed Hughie's display. 'Hereward' wrote: 'First impressions of Gallacher were distinctly favourable. No sooner did he touch the ball than one sensed the artistic player. Dwarfed in stature by the Everton backs, he had little or no chance in the air, but on the ground he showed some masterly touches. There were times when be beat three or four men by clear dribbling . . .Newcastle have found a leader of real quality.'

The crowd of 36,000 were also well pleased with the first showing of the Gallacher talent. He

Hughie, now a Tyneside hero, poses for the camera at St James' Park.

impressed the Geordie public and he knew it, saying afterwards: "Just before the match ended I realized I had been taken to the hearts of the big crowd. During a lull in play a fog-horn voice roared across the ground . . .Haway Wor Hughie." That roar was to be heard over and over again during the next five years.

Gallacher shared digs at Whitley Bay with teammates Willie Cowan, Roddie McKenzie and Joe Harris. Tyneside at that time was in severe depression, much like Lanarkshire. Unemployment was high and the General Strike was but a few months away, yet football brought smiles to the hardworking folk of the North-East.

Roddie McKenzie. Another of United's many Scots, he shared digs with Hughie.

Season 1925-6 had opened with a new offside law in which forwards reaped the benefit. The revised law, ironically due to the proficiency of an offside trap created by United backs McCracken and Hudspeth, demanded only two defenders between attackers and the goal instead of three. It resulted in a torrent of goals. A new '3-2-5' formation evolved and with it the 'stopper' centre-half. Defenders took time to adjust to the new tactics and a forward's paradise resulted. With Gallacher in their team, Newcastle were ideally placed to take advantage of the new situation as a new breed of centre-forward came to the fore to counter the third-back game — a player who was prepared to battle with the opposing centre-half and match them with wits, strength and courage. Gallacher led the way. Respected football correspondent, Ivan Sharpe, wrote of those new style centre-forwards of the day: "He manufactured his own powder and shot and couldn't be called a model . . .none had reached the all-round ability and deadliness of Hughie Gallacher." There were other goalgetters too — Middlesbrough's George Camsell, Everton's Dixie Dean, Dave Halliday at Sunderland, Joe Bradford of Birmingham and West Ham's Vic Watson to name a few.

In his first nine games in a Newcastle United shirt, Hughie scored a remarkable total of 15 goals. After the Everton match he netted against Manchester City, then weighed-in with a hat-trick against Liverpool. Four goals against Bolton Wanderers included three in the first 25 minutes. Gallacher was rapidly becoming the new idol of Tyneside. A group of United fans presented him with a medal, reserved usually for long-serving stalwarts, not individuals who had been at Gallowgate for less than two months. The hero-worship was just beginning and was to grow into the biggest that Tyneside has seen, even more fervent than Jackie Milburn's following 25 years later.

There has always been a special relationship between Newcastle United supporters and the club's centre-forwards. Up to Gallacher's joining, the Magpies fielded famous names such as Jock Peddie, Bill Appleyard, Albert Shepherd and Neil Harris. The fans adored them all. After Gallacher, a whole list of celebrated number-nines followed his tradition — Stubbins, Milburn, White, Macdonald. Both Jackie Milburn and Albert Stubbins remembered the adulation of Gallacher when they were kids, a long time after he had left United. They used to sing a song in the school playground, to the tune of *John Peel*:

'Do you 'ken Hughie Gallacher
 the wee Scots lad,
The best centre-forward
 Newcastle ever had.'
Gallacher ended the 1925-6

The Press had a field day on Tyneside with the arrival of Gallacher. Two caricatures of the Scot . . . one by 'Bos' and the other by Jimmy Seed, the former England player.

season with a hat-trick against FA Cup Finalists Manchester City on Tyneside. It was a crucial game as City needed a point to stay in the First Division. They missed a penalty, lost 3-2 and were relegated. Hughie grabbed 25 goals in only 22 appearances for Newcastle that season. Over the whole campaign, including his Scottish League games, he totalled 34 goals.

Since his transfer, Gallacher had also scored three goals in two appearances for Scotland. During February he helped send Northern Ireland to a 4-0 defeat at Ibrox Park, with another hat-trick; at the end of the season he helped Scotland defeat England 1-0 at Old Trafford. That was the 50th official match between the two countries and the sixth successive win over England for the dominant Scots. Gallacher was involved in the only goal of the game, scored by Alec Jackson. He did all the spadework in brilliant play which set up the winner. It had been quite a season for Gallacher, but nothing compared to the 12 months that were to follow.

Scotland v Ireland. Gallacher (centre) scores one of his three goals.

Scotland's team for the 50th 'Auld Enemy' international in 1926. Back row (left to right): Gibson, McMullan, official, Summers, Harper, Cunningham, official, trainer. Front: Jackson, Gallacher, McStay, Hutton, Thomson, Troup.

CHAPTER FIVE

CHAMPIONSHIP SKIPPER

"My patience and quick temper were tried to the utmost by players of lesser skill."
Hughie Gallacher

ON the eve of the 1926-7 season, Newcastle directors made a bold decision. Frank Hudspeth, full-back and veteran of over 400 games, was stripped of the captaincy and Hughie Gallacher, the whiplash import, was appointed as the black and whites' new skipper. The decision raised more than a few eyebrows. 'He is too young,' said some. 'Too inexperienced and temperamental,' said others. Gallacher had the perfect answer. His character was always one to make critics eat their words. He went on to skipper United to the League title, to date the last occasion the Tyneside club has won that princely honour.

The local Press had doubts other than the captaincy controversy. United's potential up front was questioned: 'Are United's forwards good enough?' they asked. Newcastle's front line certainly were and went on to net almost 100 goals between them, the key to United's success that year. Gallacher led the line brilliantly. Alongside him at inside-forward were two fellow Scots, former Rangers man Tom McDonald from Inverness and Bob McKay, another ex-Ibrox man who played for Scotland. Both complemented Gallacher's style perfectly,

Frank Hudspeth . . . deposed of the captaincy.

while wingers Tommy Urwin and Stan Seymour, both capped by England, were at the peaks of their careers. The five-man front line only boasted an average height of a mere 5ft 7in, yet created havoc for opposing defences.

Gallacher got off to a tremendous start. In the opening match of the season, Hughie smashed Aston Villa's offside-minded defence,

scoring all the goals as Newcastle won 4-0. For the first half of the season United looked good and were tipped in some quarters for the Championship. Gallacher's presence was the main reason. *All Sports* magazine noted: 'Gallacher is making Newcastle United a bigger power'. Following another four-goal strike by the impish leader against Bolton Wanderers, it was declared: 'What Newcastle owes to Hughie Gallacher can scarcely be overestimated. He simply covered himself with glory'. The *Newcastle Daily Journal's* scribe, 'Novocastrian', even wondered that perhaps he was superhuman: '. . .whether he did not possess more than the usual complement of feet'. Gallacher was the match-winner. For the next three seasons he was at the zenith of his career and his boundless talent showed wherever he played.

Scotland continued to select him at centre-forward. Not even Celtic's goal-ace, Jimmy McGrory, could budge Gallacher from the international team. He scored in the 3-0 victory over Wales during October, then played against England

Hughie Gallacher. United's new skipper for the 1926-7 season.

Tom McDonald, one of the Magpies five 'midget' forwards.

and Northern Ireland. The English game, in front of 111,214 fans at Hampden Park, was the first defeat for Scotland in seven games. Gallacher's teammate at Airdrie, Bob McPhail, made his debut, but it was Dixie Dean who hogged the newspaper headlines with two goals. In 12 months time it would be Scotland's turn to extract more than adequate revenge at the Empire Stadium, Wembley.

Gallacher's initial journeys to London did not impress the southern fans or the fickle London-biased media, but a visit to White Hart Lane with Newcastle during November made them all take notice. United won 3-1, Gallacher netted a brilliant hat-trick, had another three efforts go just wide of the woodwork and saw a goal disallowed. At this time Hughie was enjoying a goal-feast. He banged home seven in four matches and was on the scoresheet in five consecutive games. Yet he was not only the goal-taker, but also goal provider-in-chief. He laid on chances for both McDonald and Seymour who bagged goals by the hatful too. Gallacher possessed the natural touch, creating openings for forwards good enough to read his game. McDonald and Seymour were more than capable, closing in on the chances from midfield and the flank. By December, Newcastle were in the top three, in with the title-chasing pack of Burnley, Tottenham Hotspur, Huddersfield Town and United's North-East rivals, Sunderland.

Hughie had been in England for 12 months and now had the reputation of being the most feared striker in Division One, a forward who taunted, teased and rattled the opposing defence at times with abuse and niggling kicks and pokes. Stout defenders did not like his style one bit. Nothing can be crueller than a venomous insult about one's parentage, lack of courage, immoral way or looks, delivered in a rich Lanarkshire accent. No one had a tongue quite like Gallacher's. As a consequence he was singled out for special treatment. He had often been roughed-up in Scotland, but that was nothing to the punishment that was handed out in the First Division in England. Gallacher became a marked man. Opposing centre-halves started not only to resort to foul means to stop his forward runs, but also began to bait the Scot, knowing that his hot temper was never far from the surface. In doing so, opponents got him in trouble with referees — a tactic that worked time and time again. Gallacher recalled: "My patience and quick temper were tried to the utmost by players of lesser skill."

In virtually every match he played, much bigger defenders crashed into Gallacher without thought of possible injury to the forward. The meeting of Gallacher and centre-half was always the talking point of the game. They kicked, barged and punched him, on and off the ball. Men like Sam Cowan of Manchester City, Herbie Roberts of Arsenal, Jack Hill of Burnley — later to be a teammate of Gallacher's — Bolton's Jimmy Seddon and Sheffield United's Vince Matthews. All were internationals and all 6ft plus. Hughie was fortunate not to suffer serious injury.

Many contemporary players recalled his battle-weary body. Scotland goalkeeper Jack Harkness said: "I never saw any forward with as many scars and hacks." Dozens of times Hughie hobbled from the pitch with his legs varied in colour from blue to purple. Once he had to be taken to the railway station by taxi because he just could not walk, so harsh was the treatment. United colleague and later brother-in-law, George Mathison, remembered: "You had to see his legs to believe the treatment he was given. They were pitted, scarred. You couldn't blame him for losing his cool." And lose his cool he did. Hughie once said: "I am pretty tough, but not tough enough to knit

Herbie Roberts (top) and Sam Cowan, two of Gallacher's 6ft-plus adversaries.

wire netting or bend crowbars, or take deliberate rough usage with a smile." Tough as he was, the rough stuff affected him. Stan Seymour said that he even saw him crying in the dressing-room at half-time, from sheer frustration. Gallacher found it difficult not to explode and throw angry comments at his opponents — and the referee. He was the victim of retaliation and constantly had words with officials in charge.

Hughie, however, had to learn to live with the rough stuff as part of his game. He started wearing a half-inch thick pad of cotton wool under his shin-pads — and he tried hard to hold his frustration, no matter how difficult it was. He took the punishment with remarkable guts. He bewildered opponents by coming back again and again for more. One defender was quoted as saying: "That wee fellow was not born. He was quarried." But he could never master his temper. His Newcastle teammates even appointed Bob McKay as Gallacher's 'minder' on the field. As soon as there was a hint of trouble between players or officials, in stepped McKay to lead Gallacher from a potential flare-up. It worked only in part.

Examples of this rugged treatment are easy to find. Against Aston Villa, the comment was: 'The presence of Gallacher on the homeside appeared to be regarded as a personal affront by the Villa defenders and their efforts to hold him led to the importation of an element of roughness into their play'. At Tottenham events boiled over. The bodily attack on Gallacher led to a grave situation with a virtual free-for-all on the pitch. The origin of the trouble was the unfair tactics towards the Newcastle centre-forward. Finding ordinary methods to no avail, Tottenham did not hesitate, as it was reported, 'to resort to less reputable tactics'. The match report continued: 'Some of the contestants lost their heads in the second half and so necessitated a general warning from the referee who called all the players together'.

The continual pounding sometimes worked for him too. Against Manchester City, Hughie went on one of his famed runs, beating three men with consummate ease before Sam Cowan swept in with a reckless tackle that threw Gallacher in the air. Hughie limped away, helped by colleagues, but he had won a penalty and a resultant goal. Gallacher could never give up either — his nature never allowed him to do so.

A goal for Gallacher against Spurs at St James' Park. A flash of his head and one of his 39 goals that season is in the net.

He persisted no matter how many boots were launched at him and it often brought success. Against West Ham United during February, he opened United's account under the greatest of difficulties with tackles flying from all quarters, while his second goal was a perfect triumph of mind over matter, for he literally had to carry the attendant full-back with him, beating goalkeeper Ted Hufton with a shot that was described as 'amazing in the circumstances'.

It has to be said that while Gallacher never warranted the physical battering he received for almost ten years, his own style of play immediately goaded the opposition. The Scot would always make sure his opponent knew he was around and a rough tackle on him would be mentally remembered. In that match against Tottenham, Jack Elkes of Spurs dished out a few particularly nasty fouls. Gallacher returned the compliment later in the match and Elkes had to retire to the touchline for lengthy treatment. The *Newcastle Daily Journal* went to great length debating this part of Gallacher's game and its consequences. In summing up, it was, 'a price which is the unavoidable penalty of greatness'.

Despite all the bruises and abuse from players and away fans alike, who loved to hate the centre-forward, Hughie battled on. He missed only four games for the Magpies in the 1926-7 season. As the New Year opened, Newcastle hit top form. They went to the top of the table following a run which saw them record six wins in a row. They also started well in the FA Cup, with an 8-1 thrashing of Notts County at St James' Park, Gallacher scoring a hat-trick in the first half, even though he was handicapped by a temperature of 102° F just before the kick-off. That game featured another of his finest goals, balancing the ball on his head for a few seconds before allowing it to drop and

volleying home. In addition, the spectacle of Wee Hughie, at 5ft 5in, up against Notts goalkeeper Albert Iremonger, 6ft 5½in and 13½st, was an amazing sight.

The Tynesiders continued in fine form, defeating famous public school and university combination, The Corinthians, in the FA Cup before being surprisingly knocked out by Southampton in the fifth round. But their League form did not desert the side. Gallacher went on the rampage. Against Everton, 45,000 saw United win 7-3 with three goals from the Scotsman, the first of ten goals in a six-match spell

which set the Magpies up nicely for the title. Included in those goals was another Gallacher classic, this time at Ewood Park against Blackburn Rovers.

Stan Seymour reckoned it was the greatest Gallacher scored for Newcastle United. He recounted the goal: "I remember I passed the ball to Hughie and sent him off on a 30-yard dribble down the wing. I tore down the middle. The goalkeeper came out to narrow the angle, expecting, like me, that Hughie would send the ball over as I had a clear shot at goal. That was too simple. Hughie pushed the ball

League Champions in 1927. United's line-up proudly display the trophy. Gallacher is in the centre, next to the Championship trophy and chairman John Oliver.

gently through the goalkeeper's legs." It was typical Gallacher. He would never be afraid to try the unexpected and spectacular. Most times he succeeded — the mark of his genius.

The title race was now between three clubs: United, Huddersfield Town, winners of the Championship for the previous three seasons, and Sunderland. United met their North-East foes in a decisive clash during March. A record attendance was attracted to St James' Park, where 67,211 fans watched the top and second-placed clubs meet. A goal by Gallacher – who else? – was

enough to seal the points. It sent United into the Easter fixtures in confident mood and to an equally crucial double with Huddersfield Town.

Another massive crowd packed into United's Gallowgate stadium when 62,500 saw the battle of challengers v holders. Once more Hughie Gallacher was the ace in the pack. Just after half-time he headed into the net from a brilliant neck-twisting effort after Seymour had nodded the ball across goal from a move started by McKay. Hughie was challenged by Tom Wilson, who stood 6ft, and to the end of his days

the Huddersfield Town centre-half could never explain how Gallacher outjumped him. Although Town won the return match 1-0, Newcastle were almost there.

They defeated Spurs 3-2 and needed only a point from a trip to Upton Park on 23 April. United drew 1-1 with the Hammers and were hailed as champions at St James' Park seven days later, when United entertained Sheffield Wednesday. Gallacher netted both goals in a 2-1 victory to bring his tally to 39 in 41 games for the season. A new club record was established, one that still stands,

over 60 years later. Hughie just missed becoming the division's top goalscorer – Sheffield Wednesday's Jimmy Trotter gaining that honour by a single goal.

Skipper Gallacher had answered his critics. So too had United's forward line. Apart from Gallacher, Tom McDonald knocked in 23 goals and Seymour 19, a club record for a winger. The Magpies' home form had been outstanding and their 19 wins from 21 matches has been equalled only once, by Liverpool during the 1970s. They possessed not only the best attack in the country, but also the sternest defensive record too. Deposed captain, Frank Hudspeth, marshalled the rearguard. Charlie Spencer, at centre-half, was capped along with Hudspeth, although he was almost 36 years old. Alf Maitland was impressive at full-back and Scottish goalkeeper Willie Wilson proved a safe last line of defence. Willie Gibson and Roddie McKenzie were two powerful wing-halves and two more men from north of the border. They possessed a wonderful team spirit led by the irrepressible Gallacher. The *Northern Echo Football Annual* summed up: 'In Hughie Gallacher, their centre-forward and captain, they possess a footballer and leader who stands alone in the matter of skill. It was largely due to his brilliance and the support he derived from his colleagues that Newcastle United gained the League honours.'

It was a marvellous year for the North-East all round. Apart from United's success, Sunderland finished third, while Middlesbrough were Second Division champions. Everywhere the talk was of football and nobody loved it more than Hughie Gallacher. Idolized, he marched proudly round the pubs and working-mens' clubs of Tyneside and was dubbed the best-

(opposite, bottom): Autographs from United's successful team. Top to bottom: Seymour, Urwin, Hudspeth, Spencer, McDonald, Wilson, McKay, Gibson, Maitland, McKenzie and Hughie Gallacher.

(top): Gallacher's jersey for that season. Football League Division One table for 1927

DIVISION 1							1926-27
1	Newcastle	42	25	6	11	96:58	56
2	Huddersfield	42	17	17	8	76:60	51
3	Sunderland	42	21	7	14	98:70	49
4	Bolton	42	19	10	13	84:62	48
5	Burnley	42	19	9	14	91:80	47
6	West Ham	42	19	8	15	86:70	46
7	Leicester	42	17	12	13	85:70	46
8	Sheffield U.	42	17	10	15	74:86	44
9	Liverpool	42	18	7	17	69:61	43
10	Aston Villa	42	18	7	17	81:83	43
11	The Arsenal	42	17	9	16	77:86	43
12	Derby	42	17	7	18	86:73	41
13	Tottenham	42	16	9	17	76:78	41
14	Cardiff	42	16	9	17	55:65	41
15	Manchester U.	42	13	14	15	52:64	40
16	The Wednesday	42	15	9	18	75:92	39
17	Birmingham	42	17	4	21	64:73	38
18	Blackburn	42	15	8	19	77:96	38
19	Bury	42	12	12	18	68:77	36
20	Everton	42	12	10	20	64:90	34
21	Leeds	42	11	8	23	69:88	30
22	West Bromwich	42	11	8	23	65:86	30

dressed young man in the North. Smartly turned out in well-tailored suits and white spats, he often wore a white hat or a bowler and tightly-rolled umbrella — a complete 1920s dandy. He opened garden parties, graced dances with his presence and adored being recognized and signing autographs. The razzmatazz was made for him. He loved showing off and even flashed wads of money — much of it neatly cut from worthless paper with a few notes on top. He took taxis everywhere, even for the

(above): Footballers 1920s style. United's party en route for a match. Gallacher is in the centre of the front row with bowler hat and spats. Other players and officials are (left to right): Watt junior (assistant secretary), Seymour, Land, Spencer, Wilson (behind), Gibson, Gallacher, Maitland (behind), McKenzie, McDonald, Hudspeth.

(below): 'Tot' Anderson, prominent local licensee and Hughie's future father-in-law.

shortest of journeys, just to be seen in a high-class style. Hughie lived life to the full. He accepted drinks from friends and fans eager to speak to him and enjoyed the charms of adoring Newcastle women. But, despite all the outward signs of a rich and successful man, he always had feeling for the underprivileged. Hughie was a soft-hearted individual and a kind character. Once when he was waiting for a train at Newcastle Central Station he saw a poor-looking soul huddled in a corner. Over Gallacher went, took off his expensive overcoat and gave it to the man, one of the city's down and outs.

He met the second lady in his life on one of those nights out with fellow players Tommy Lang, Roddie McKenzie and Jimmy Boyd. He was introduced to the 17-year-old daughter of the landlord of

41

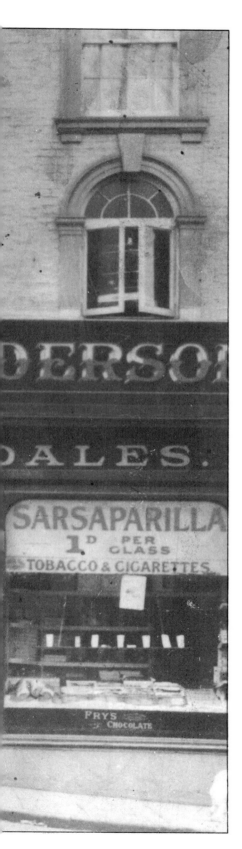

The William IV public house, one of 'Tot' Anderson's establishments and a regular haunt of Gallacher's.

an hotel in Gateshead whose bar was a favourite of United's players. She was Hannah Anderson, one of seven daughters. Her father, 'Tot' Anderson, was a well-known character and licensee, prominent United supporter and promotor of various sporting functions. 'Tot' organized dog racing, curling and later became a director of Gateshead FC. He looked after several bars — The William IV in Bottle Bank, The Anchor, The Three Bulls and The Nag's Head. All became Gallacher's chosen haunts. Hughie was constantly in Hannah's company, but never mentioned that he was still married. When the Anderson family found out, Hannah's brother had it out with Hughie. The result was a confrontation under the flickering gas lights of the High Level Bridge which crosses the Tyne, and a subsequent court appearance. Both men were bound over to keep the peace.

The romance flourished, though, and much later they were married when Gallacher was at Chelsea. Another United teammate, reserve wing-half George Mathison also found a wife from the Anderson family. He married Hannah's sister, Annie. Also married into the clan was one-time boxing champion Will Curley. He was later involved with the St James' Boxing Hall, a frequent retreat of United's players.

Gallacher lived hard and was constantly out dining, drinking and socializing. But he never forgot his football, the game which put him where he was. He trained equally hard and would never let it be said that his life off the field affected his game in any way whatsoever.

Gallacher — he had answered his critics in the best possible way.

CHAPTER SIX

A WEMBLEY WIZARD

'Scotland's whole team played with a dominant mastery that was made to appear sheer effrontery.'
Daily Mail

THE Scottish national team possessed countless footballing 'immortals' during the 1920s. The early part of the decade saw England defeat the Scots only once and, when the 1927-8 season started, Scotland boasted a sensational postwar record. In 24 games since 1919 they had produced 17 wins, three draws and only four defeats. They held superior status over Northern Ireland and Wales and especially over The Auld Enemy, England, the only match of the Home International Championship that really mattered. The Scotland team included names such as Davie Meiklejohn, Andy Cunningham, Andy Wilson and Alan Morton. Hughie Gallacher entered the action in 1924 and had appeared in ten internationals so far. He had scored nine goals and been on the losing side once, against England in 1927.

The game against Wales in October produced a 2-2 draw, with Scotland 2-0 ahead after 15 minutes through Gallacher and a Jock Hutton penalty. Bob McKay was capped alongside his Newcastle skipper in that game. Gallacher missed the next match, against the Irish, with Jimmy McGrory, prolific scorer north of the border, depu-

tizing. The Scots fell 1-0 and all was not well in the tartan camp. Changes were made for the clash with England at Wembley in March. Seasoned internationals like Hutton, McStay and Meiklejohn were omitted, McPhail and Cunningham overlooked. Tommy Law and 'Tiny' Bradshaw won their first caps, Alex James only his second. Gallacher returned, despite the fact he had not kicked a ball for two months, and this caused uproar in Glasgow as Celtic's McGrory was dropped in his favour. It was a raw-looking team and a criticized one, for it contained eight Anglos and only three home-based players. Yet both individually and together, the blend was perfect. On the day, each man was the master of his job, all thoughtful and creative and each worked for the team. There were 80,868 at Wembley for the match against England on that day, the afternoon the legend of the Wembley Wizards was born. The two teams lined up in front of the Duke of York and his guest, King Amanullah of Afghanistan, as follows:

England: E.Hufton (West Ham U); F.Goodhall (Huddersfield T), H.Jones (Blackburn R),

W.Edwards(Leeds U), T.Wilson (Huddersfield T), H.Healless (Blackburn R), J.Hulme (Arsenal), R.Kelly (Huddersfield T), W.Dean (Everton), J.Bradford (Birmingham), W.Smith (Huddersfield T).

Scotland: J.Harkness (Queen's Park); J.Nelson (Cardiff C), T.Law (Chelsea), J.Gibson (Aston Villa), T.Bradshaw (Bury), J.McMullan (Manchester C), A.Jackson (Huddersfield T), J.Dunn (Hibernian), H.Gallacher (Newcastle U), A.James (Preston NE), A. Morton (Rangers).

It was only the second England-Scotland meeting at the Empire Stadium and Hughie Gallacher's first visit to Wembley. On a soaked, lush turf the complete and utter defeat of the English was seen — a display to earn the 11 Scotsmen immortality. It was said that captain Jimmy McMullan prayed for rain which would suit their diminutive forward line — only winger Alex Jackson, at 5ft 10in, was what could be described as tall — James, Gallacher, Morton and Dunn were barely 5ft 6in. When the teams arrived at Wembley it was raining — pouring torrents on to the pitch. It was to be Scotland's day.

The England side were bewildered by the Scots' football. Scotland's pace, interplay and goalscoring shone in dazzling style. The *Daily Mail* commented: 'Scotland's whole team played with a dominant mastery that was made to appear sheer effrontery'. Gallacher held the line with perfection and was in place to get his forwards moving at all

The Duke of York, later King George VI, meets the Scottish players before the England game. Left to right: Dunn, Gallacher, Jackson, Gibson, Harkness, Nelson, Bradshaw.

Hughie Gallacher, Newcastle's and Scotland's best.

An attempt at goal by Gallacher. England defenders Goodall, Jones and goalkeeper Ted Hufton watch anxiously but the effort went just past the post.

times, pushing, coaxing the ball as if it belonged to him. He was joined by his old school pal, Alex James, and winger Alec Jackson. They were dubbed 'The Three Musketeers', and their skills were complementary. On the other flank Alan Morton was simply superb, while skipper McMullan, another 'midget genius', was the commanding influence from midfield.

England hit the post in the first few minutes, but Scotland's goals came quickly. From the rebound of that English near miss, McMullan set up the first for the Scots, Jackson heading home with Gallacher involved in the move. The Huddersfield Town winger, later a teammate of Hughie's at Chelsea, went on to score a hat-trick and tormented left-back Bert Jones. James netted a couple, one brilliantly set up by Hughie as he went on a typical run. Scotland's leader did not get on to the score-sheet but had played his

part, as did every member of the Scots team in the 5-1 victory. The Wembley Wizards 'gave an exhibition of scientific football that was a revelation', as one English critic wrote. Amazingly, that very team never played together again.

It was revealed after the match that Gallacher had played the full 90 minutes with his mind not totally on football. He was worried by problems at home in Scotland and afterwards was informed that his brother's wife had died before the

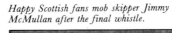

Happy Scottish fans mob skipper Jimmy McMullan after the final whistle.

Alan Morton, one of Gallacher's Wizard colleagues.

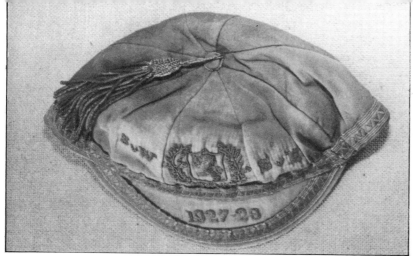

The immortal Wizards cap . . . Scotland v England 1927-8.
Match-day programme, 31 March 1928.

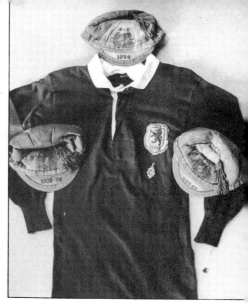

Gallacher's Wembley Wizards shirt, together with
international caps; Scotland v Ireland 1924 (top),
v Wales 1929-30 (left), v Wales 1926-7 (right).

THE FOOTBALL ASSOCIATION
INTERNATIONAL MATCH

Stadium Wembley
March 31st 1928

ENGLAND
v
SCOTLAND

The valve with the wonderful Mullard P.M. Filament.

Mullard
THE MASTER-VALVE

OFFICIAL PROGRAMME   **PRICE SIX PENCE**

PL   D & PUBLISHED BY FRED. E. BLOWER & CO. 152, HIGH ST. WATFORD

game, the bad news being kept from him. There were no real celebrations for Gallacher as he hurried to catch the first train north.

The reason Hughie Gallacher almost missed that famous and historic Wembley occasion was a two-month suspension by the football authorities, due to continued altercations with defenders and, more important, referees. Knowing his temperament was on a very short fuse, defenders would work on him, niggling him wherever he went until his temper erupted. He often became involved in skirmishes and just as often got a finger-wagging from referees. But Hughie could never stop the debate. Most players are clever enough to save any remarks to the referee until he is out of earshot. Gallacher could not do that. Venomous words would chastise the man in charge, and he paid the penalty. He recorded later in his career: "I realize I should have made greater efforts to hold my tongue."

In refereeing circles he had a reputation. Gallacher said: "I was a regular topic among them and some I'm sure judged me before I set foot on the pitch." He constantly complained — justifiably in some cases — about rough treatment. But that was not all. He would argue about most decisions: free-kicks,

47

Bert Fogg. An incident with Gallacher led to a two-month suspension for Hughie.

throw-ins and especially penalty claims. It was one such spot-kick appeal that got him into big trouble on New Year's Eve 1927, in a needle game against Huddersfield Town, the club Newcastle had pipped to the Championship the year before.

United had emphatically beaten the Yorkshire side on the opening day of the season, when Gallacher

Gallacher . . . a fine action study.

started with a hat-trick, and the Magpie's striker took some harsh treatment from Town's defenders in the return game at St James' Park. Throughout the match he persistently complained to referee Bert Fogg, one of the country's top officials. Before the game, Fogg had told both sets of players that, due to the hard and frosty surface, he would not tolerate heavy challenges. When the game started, the referee

did not live up to his word and this incensed Hughie, perhaps justly so, as he was on the receiving end. His complaining, however, was to no avail and in the closing minutes, Huddersfield went ahead 3-2 with a penalty, a 'diabolical' decision according to home fans and one that upset Gallacher immensely. Moments later the Newcastle leader was felled in the box by Redfern — "Penalty!" he yelled, but referee Fogg would have none of it, despite the waving of a linesman's flag. Gallacher lost his cool completely

and howled at the Bolton official in vociferous Lanarkshire dialect. He continued to do so for the few minutes remaining.

The referee threatened to book him, and said: "What's your name?" Hughie replied, annoyed: "If you don't know that you have no business being on the field." He added: "And what's your name?" The referee replied: "I'm Mr Fogg." Hughie quickly jumped in, with a

Newcastle United in 1927. Back row (left to right): Clark, Curry, Harris, Spencer, McKenzie, Low, Lang. Front: Watt (secretary), Urwin, McKay, Hudspeth, Gallacher, Maitland, McDonald, Seymour, McPherson (trainer). On ground: Wilson.

grin: "Yes, and you've been in one all the afternoon." As the players trooped off, Hughie could still be seen wagging his finger at the referee. Stan Seymour related that Gallacher was furious, the worst he had ever seen him. A friend of Hughie's recorded what happened in the dressing-room: "Hughie

Kilt and bagpipes for this caricature of Scotland's centre-forward.

approached Mr Fogg after the match with an intent to apologise. He found the official bending over to go into the bath — Hughie kicked out and pushed him in. He just couldn't resist it!"

Mr Fogg was not amused. Gallacher had crossed swords with the same referee before and on this occasion Fogg reported the Scot to the FA in the strongest terms. On 20 January it was announced that Hughie Gallacher had been given a two-month suspension. The FA said that it was 'for improper conduct both on the field and at the close of this match, and so having regard to his misconduct in previous matches'. It was a severe penalty that shocked everyone in the game. He was not even allowed a personal hearing at the Disciplinary Committee. Hughie asked the question in *The Journal:* "Why did the FA refuse my request for a personal hearing of the charges made against me? I have not been fairly treated." He felt strongly that he was pronounced guilty without a trial, an early indication of Football Association and Football League power that was to cause major problems to football some 40 years later.

Gallacher was out of the game for two months. He could not train with Newcastle, he received no wages and spent the period back in Bellshill. He was offered a contract by a Glasgow newspaper to comment on Scottish Cup ties — and made more money than his football wage would have been.

But for this controversy it would have been another wonderful year for Gallacher personally. Before the season started he was offered big money to play in the United States for the Fall River Club, but did not relish the standard of football much. With Newcastle, Hughie hit 11 goals in his first 11 games as the Magpies started like champions. But the team's form did not progress, although Gallacher continued to find the net, getting 21 goals in 33 games. One was through the legs of respected England goalkeeper Harry Hibbs of Birmingham, a memory Hughie always cherished. Of Gallacher's football talent, Hibbs later said: "The best I have ever met."

Gallacher holds off a defender in a tussle for the ball.

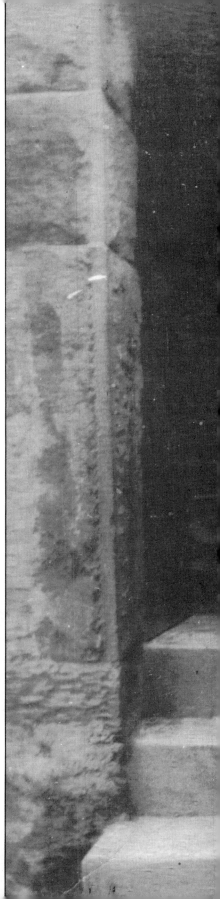

Hughie in civvies – as smart as they come.

CHAPTER SEVEN

DRUNK . . . . IN CHARGE OF A FOOTBALL

"It was a boiling hot day so we rinsed our mouths out with a drop of Scotch and water."
Alf Maitland

HUGHIE Gallacher's brush with officialdom caused a serious rift between himself and certain members of the New-castle United club. At that time the Magpies, like most sides, had not yet been adventurous enough to appoint a full-time team boss, playing affairs being solely the responsibility of the directors. Some members of the board were clearly unhappy at the Scot's clash with the Football Association and Football League and his seemingly uncontrollable temper. They wanted to get rid of him, sources said. Speculation was heightened when Arsenal manager, Herbert Chapman, turned up at St James' Park at the beginning of the season. Rumours circulated rapidly that Gallacher was heading south to Highbury. But the majority of the men in charge insisted that a talent which had netted 85 goals in two and a half seasons was too valuable to lose. However, Gallacher was stripped of the captaincy before the new season began. Fellow Scottish international, Joe Harris from Glasgow, a player of a more placid nature,

Hill v Gallacher. A typical meeting in an England v Scotland clash.

Gallacher, relieved of the captaincy at Newcastle.

was handed the job, albeit for a short while. Gallacher had been reprimanded. He was to stay out of trouble and concentrate on his job in football — scoring goals.

Newcastle had a mediocre season by their standards and, come the winter months, were struggling at the foot of the table. All was not well in the camp. The directors had a 'clear-out' before the New Year. Players came and went and it was reported that Alex James was about to join Gallacher on Tyneside. It was Hughie who nobbled James when the pair met back home in Bellshill.

James was then with Preston North End and was keen to move. However, Newcastle's directors considered the Mossend inside-forward too small, an amazing judgement considering Gallacher's contribution. They hesitated and James signed for Arsenal, to the Geordies' loss.

One player to arrive at St James' Park, though, was one of Gallacher's great antagonists, centre-half Jack Hill, captain of Burnley and England. The pair had clashed many times and the Gallacher-Hill duel, 5ft 5in against 6ft 2in, was one of

the most talked about in football at the time. Every time they met, whether at club or international level, there was great expectation at the confrontation. Hill once hit Gallacher like a ton of bricks in a clash with Burnley and Hughie never forgot it. One match commentator recorded a meeting in September 1926. Jack Hill was in a stern mood: 'His robust duels with Gallacher aroused a feverish temperament and after both had been penalized for the illegitimate practice of physical force they were personally addressed by the referee who administered a significant caution'.

Hill was a fabulous stopper and one of the few men who could actually tame Gallacher. In a Burnley-United clash in 1928-9 the Scot became so frustrated and fed up with the powerful Durham-born centre-half that he walked off the field, although he was quickly persuaded to return by trainer Jimmy McPherson. Newcastle were desperate for a defender to replace Charlie Spencer, not to mention a commanding skipper. Gallacher was asked for his opinion by United's chairman, Mr John Oliver: "Who would you recommend, Hughie?" The Newcastle boss gasped when Gallacher replied with Hill's name, his number-one foe. "Hill can hold me and if he can do that to me he'll master any centre-forward in the country." The red-haired defender joined United for £8,100, a new record transfer. Hill said later: "Actually, Hughie and I were the best of pals. We had tough clashes, true, but we took them in the right spirit. And when I joined Newcastle on his recommendation, we were almost inseparable."

Changes at St James' Park brought better results and the Tynesiders recovered in the remaining months of the season to finish tenth. There was quite a Scots influence at Gallowgate then. Indeed, it was more like a Saturday at Glasgow Cross than in the north-east of England. Once in that season,

Jack Hill, one of Gallacher's great opponents, now United's captain.

54

Scotland's team against England in 1929. Alec Cheyne replaced Tom Muirhead at the last moment and netted the winning goal.

Newcastle fielded a line-up against Leeds United that did not contain one Englishman. There were ten Scots in the side, the odd man out being centre-half, Ed Wood, a Welshman.

Hughie was in good company and never once became homesick. Both Tommy Lang and Willie Gibson came from Larkhall, not far from Bellshill, and reserve forward Willie Chalmers was born a goal-kick from Hughie's house in that Lanarkshire town. Glasgow was represented by Bob McKay, Joe Harris and Gallacher's best pal, Jimmy Boyd, later capped by Scotland. Goalkeeper Willie Wilson hailed from Edinburgh, Tom McDonald from Inverness and Jimmy Low from Ayrshire. It was home from home.

Hughie had kept out of trouble for most of the season. He had another profitable goalscoring year, being United's top scorer once more, this time with 24 goals. He hit the headlines in a blue shirt for Scotland — perhaps his best year for his country — scoring no fewer than eight times in the Scots' three games. Against Wales in October he registered a hat-trick in a 4-2 win at Ibrox Park. A crowd of 55,000 saw Gallacher in marvellous form. Wales were in front at half-time through an early goal, but immediately after the break, Gallacher struck and the Scots found themselves 3-1 ahead.

That victory was followed by a crushing 7-3 win against Northern Ireland in Belfast and Gallacher caught all the praise again. His display against the Irish was even more resounding — a hat-trick in the first quarter of the game and five goals altogether. He combined a treat with Alec Jackson, who made five of the Scots' seven goals as well as getting two himself. It was the Gallacher and Jackson show. Hughie's five was a Scottish record,

Hughie (right) watches Alec Cheyne's corner find the net in the meeting with England in 1929. Hacking can only watch.

Gallacher in action with England goalkeeper Jack Hacking at Hampden Park.

although several sources only gave him four goals, with James claiming one of his strikes. However, the centre-forward had no doubt. He said: "Several newspapers mistakenly credited Alex James with one of my scoring efforts." The referee for that match was none other than Bert Fogg. Gallacher, after the incident at St James' Park the previous season, turned it on. The two met up at an hotel and the Lancastrian said to Gallacher: "You know, Hughie, a referee's job is a hard one at times." Hughie agreed.

The big match of the year, England v Scotland, was staged at Hampden Park. Hughie almost missed the game, injured for the preceeding fortnight. Dave Halliday of Sunderland was pencilled in at centre-forward but Gallacher was preferred, even though he was not fully fit. A crowd of 110,512 saw Scotland defeat the Sassenachs 1-0, with only ten men, as Jackson was off for a long period with a dislocated elbow. Gallacher was involved in the goal — a controversial one. New cap Alec Cheyne hit a corner kick in the dying minutes. The cross swirled in the wind and the ball ended up in the net. England defenders claimed that Hughie had stood on goalkeeper John Hacking's foot, so preventing the Oldham Athletic man from clearing the ball. Gallacher was back in the news.

It was at the end of the season that the mercurial centre-forward got himself into trouble again, after almost a year of good behaviour. He was caught in a set-to with a referee. Once again it was a case of back-chat to the official, but this time Gallacher was lucky — the FA gave him a severe warning but no suspension. Later, to augment his income, Hughie wrote a series of newspaper articles. They were called 'Inside the Football Game' and, of course, were controversial. The FA were displeased and censured him again. They fined Gallacher £5 and instructed the Newcastle player to end his writing, alleging that the column was 'causing dissatisfaction in more than one dressing-room.'

Following that, Gallacher was off on tour with his club and into more confrontation. Newcastle embarked on a European trek during May 1929, visiting Italy, Czechoslovakia, Hungary and Austria. They won their first game, 1-0 against Ambrosiana Milan, but it was an experience United's party wanted to forget. The Italians resorted to tactics more familiar to a rugby field or a boxing ring. United's players limped off the field with Tommy Lang, hardly ever one to lose his cool, being sent off along with his opposing full-back. Lang later showed his colleagues a nasty set of bite marks on his neck. United, to say the least, did not give an exhibition display. They 'mixed it' too and the crowd did not like it. After the game a mob gathered round the club's coach. Stones and bottles whizzed through the windows. Skipper 'Ginger' Hill, Dave Fairhurst and reserve goalkeeper Micky Burns were all hit. Gallacher noted in his memoirs: "Frankly I was scared stiff and never more glad to see cops in my life." Those policemen were the blackshirt guard of Mussolini. There was more trouble at the Magpies' hotel, United's players having to barricade themselves in bedrooms, and only the intervention of a member of the Italian Government — who was staying at the same hotel — together with the British Consul, stopped another dust-up developing.

The tour turned sour after that unpleasant opening. Against WAC Vienna, United lost 2-0 and then came an embarrassing 8-1 defeat at the hands of Slovak Czechoslovakia, after which Czech officials accused the Geordies of not trying. United travelled to Budapest to meet an Hungarian XI in a match that almost blew up into an international incident with Hughie Gallacher at the centre of it. The game was another rough 90 minutes

Newcastle United pictured on their Continental tour in 1929. Back row (left to right): Maitland, Curry, Hudspeth, Wilson, Spencer, McKenzie. Front: Urwin, Clarke, Gallacher, McDonald, Seymour.

and Hughie said of Continental football, which he experienced for the first time: "Their skill was at an absolute minimum and the only way they could stop us was by the crudest tactics imaginable."

Newcastle lost 4-1, Gallacher netting a penalty. United full-back

Alf Maitland was sent off and then Gallacher received his marching orders after a punch-up with the home full-back. As the Scot trooped off, fans spat and threw coins at him. He was taken through the seething crowd by armed soldiers. Hungarian officials and players were incensed. They accused United's players — Gallacher in particular — of being drunk and disorderly on the field. They withheld Newcastle's

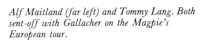
Alf Maitland (far left) and Tommy Lang. Both sent-off with Gallacher on the Magpie's European tour.

(bottom, left): Gallacher . . . brought before the FA with his Newcastle teammates.

(below): Hughie relaxing on the beach with his pet dog.

guaranteed payment, claiming that they did not deserve any fee because the players were intoxicated and not willing to display football. A strong complaint went to the English FA. Newcastle were quick to leave the country.

Back on British soil, a full FA enquiry took place at Lancaster Gate to investigate the Budapest incident. Gallacher was at the centre of attention again. This time the FA allowed Hughie to give his point of view. In the end they accepted his explanation and officially exoner-ated him, although the damage to his reputation had already been done. Gallacher explained that he, and some of his teammates, had been so thirsty that they had washed their mouths out with whisky, hence the alcoholic breath. Alf Maitland backed Hughie, saying: "It was a boiling hot day so we rinsed our mouths out with a drop of Scotch and water." The United full-back also said that the Hungarians had seen them passing the bottle round and spread the word to the crowd that they were drunk. From the kick-off, the crowd were booing and howling.

The all-powerful FA came down on the side of Newcastle United who received their match fee from the Hungarians. However, it had been an extremely harmful controversy and one that put Gallacher's track record with certain Newcastle officials on a worse standing.

The 1929-30 season about to start was to be Hughie Gallacher's last with Newcastle United. Just before the big kick-off in August, he asked for a transfer and was

linked with both Arsenal and Tottenham. A week before, United had signed Duncan Hutchison, another Scot, from Dundee United — a centre-forward with a good reputation, who had just crashed 40 goals in one season for the Tay club. Gallacher saw the purchase as his replacement, especially when it was suggested that he would be handed the centre-forward's role with Gallacher being pushed inside. Fierce debate raged. Gallacher was still King of Tyneside. The club's directors dare not transfer him; they backed down and disagreements were patched up, Hughie signing another year's contract. However, the rift between the club

and player was broader. It was not to be healed.

In spite of the transfer speculation, Gallacher started on top of his game, as if to show Newcastle officials what they would miss. He scored three goals on the first Saturday of the season, in a 4-1 win over Manchester United, and netted 11 goals in the first ten games. His scoring prowess, however, could not stop the Gallowgate side sliding to 18th place. It was to be a relegation-threatened season for United, and Gallacher, with his goals — he bagged 34 — saved them from the drop.

No one gave more for the Magpies that season. Hughie's

commitment was unquestioned, although his loyalty to his club got him into more confrontation. Gallacher just could not win. Whenever he hit the headlines it upset someone. A 'club v country' row blew up during April when Gallacher decided to play for Newcastle in a vital relegation clash against Arsenal, rather than turn out for Scotland against England. He had impressed again in the blue

During Gallacher's last season on Tyneside, United reached the FA Cup Sixth Round. They fell to Hull City in a replay, The Hull Daily Mail *portrays the game and 'Gallacher's disappointment'. Hull scorer, Jimmy Howieson, was a former colleague at Airdrie.*

jersey that season, against Wales and Northern Ireland, scoring two goals in each victory. One at Ninian Park stood out as brilliant — it was said that he went past no fewer than eight men before scoring.

Hughie was Scotland's key player. In the last five internationals he had lashed 12 goals for his country and was selected for the England clash, but was asked by United's directors to sacrifice his cap. Hughie decided his duty lay with his club and was replaced by Fleming of Rangers. The Scots received a 5-2 hammering at Wembley. United drew 1-1 with Arsenal. The Gunners were also in trouble at the wrong end of the table, but they had released their Scots gem, Alex James, for the prestige international, together with England's David Jack. Gallacher's presence for Newcastle was crucial. He made the goal for Devine to earn United an equalizer and a vital point.

On the eve of the fixture, a Football League meeting was called to discuss the very problem Gallacher had found himself in, the 'club or country' dilemma. A resolution was passed calling for the FA to change rules relating to players' release in the clubs' favour. A row continued which eventually led to the Scottish FA deciding they would only pick home-based players. Soon Gallacher and his like, names like James, Gibson and McMullan, could not play for Scotland as long as they remained in England.

Newcastle's fight to avoid relegation lasted to the very last day of the season and a game against West Ham on 3 May 1930. It was to be Hughie Gallacher's last appearance in a Newcastle shirt, although nobody knew it then. A dramatic Joe Devine goal, watched by 50,000, ensured First Division survival. Prior to the match, another row between Hughie and the club flared up.

Reports circulated that the star centre-forward had been offered to deadly rivals, Sunderland, for a record fee. Denials were swift and profuse, but the local newspaper which released the story stuck to its words. Gallacher was amazed at Newcastle United's attitude. He had signed a new contract for the 1930-31 season but, within a few hours, he was apparently being offered to the Roker Park club. Newcastle denied the claims but Hughie was adamant and was to record: "I *had* been offered to the Sunderland club." He was vexed and said: "No one has ever shown the door to Hughie Gallacher twice. I am not a pawn to be transferred willy nilly."

It appeared that the majority of the Newcastle board now wanted to be rid of the player. The club had now appointed a manager, former Rangers and Scotland ace, Andy Cunningham. Gallacher admitted that he was never on the best of terms with the tall Glaswegian. He said to a pal: "Once Cunningham arrived as boss I knew my days were numbered at Newcastle United." Nothing came of the Sunderland move, nor of an alleged approach by a London club. Gallacher said: "I know nothing whatsoever about enquiries concerning me." That club turned out to be Chelsea. Hughie made it clear that he did not wish to leave St James' Park and was being pushed out the door. He was proud to be a Newcastle player and had a fondness for Tyneside. United fans still worshipped him. Petitions, letters and irate callers flooded the club and Press. They, on no account, wanted Gallacher to be transferred.

The incident died down, with Gallacher officially a United player again for 1930-31. Immediately the 1929-30 season ended, he travelled with the Scottish party to meet France. While he was impressing the French public and sightseeing in Paris, negotiations on Tyneside were taking place behind his back to make him a Chelsea player. This after five years as Newcastle United's top scorer and with over 140 goals behind him in a black and white shirt.

Andy Cunningham, Newcastle's new manager who never saw eye-to-eye with Gallacher.

CHAPTER EIGHT

THE DEEP SOUTH AND CHELSEA

"Why Newcastle wanted to let me go I never found out. But with such an attitude I was bound to leave the club."
Hughie Gallacher

Scotland before their meeting with France in 1930. Back row (left to right): Nelson, Thomson, Wilson, Walker, Hill, Crapnell. Front: Jackson, Cheyne, Gallacher, Stevenson, Connor.

THE Colombes Stadium in Paris was a marvellous setting for Scotland's first match against a foreign nation. The date was 18 May 1930 and the French loved the sight of Hughie Gallacher in full flight. 'Vive Le Gallacher,' the 25,000 crowd shouted as he smashed the ball past the home goalkeeper Thépot on two occasions, one in each half, to give the Scots a 2-0 victory. It was an easy win and the French 'keeper was solely responsible for saving his side from a five or six-goal drubbing, and for preventing Gallacher grabbing even more goals.

Hughie was thrilled at the reception given to him and aimed to enjoy his week-long stay in France, seeing the sights and sampling the Paris night-life. However, he again found himself in hot water. Scotland's players were under strict orders to stay in the hotel after a certain hour and, it was said, even to have their bedroom doors locked. But Gallacher and one or two of his team-mates had other ideas. They climbed out of the hotel windows and went on the town. Hughie and company were severely reprimanded for their conduct.

Back on British shores, Gallacher

headed for Bellshill now the football season was over. On Empire Day, 24 May, his relaxation was interrupted when an unexpected knock at the door brought him face to face with two officials of Chelsea Football Club, chairman Claude Kirby and scout Jock Fraser. Gallacher was surprised and astounded at the call. He told the Chelsea representatives he had no intention of signing for Chelsea or moving south: "I don't particularly want to go and surely you are overstepping the limit approaching me like this." Then came the shattering words to Hughie: "Newcastle United have agreed terms with us." He was shocked that the Tyneside club had let him go. He loved the North-East and its folk and did not want to leave.

He felt stabbed in the back and said later: "Why Newcastle wanted to let me go I never found out. But

Gallacher, a carricature by Jos Walker, now on his way to Stamford Bridge after 143 goals for Newcastle.

United fans' tribute to Gallacher . . . in verse.

with such an attitude I was bound to leave the club. Better sooner than later." Together with the Chelsea officials, the dapper Scot travelled to Glasgow, dressed in a smart suit and bowler hat, to meet Newcastle's party at a top hotel. Gallacher could have refused the move. He had, only a matter of weeks before, signed a new contract with the Magpies but now, knowing that his club would rather be without him, there was no use staying.

Negotiations were not easy, though. Hughie drove a hard bargain. He recalled in a newspaper column: "We started negotiating at 11 o'clock in the morning. Afternoon came and went. So did tea

"Hugh Gallagher."
(Formerly of Newcastle United, now of Chelsea).

1
There's a canny little lad,
Who once made all Tyneside glad,
He's the greatest living player in the game
He's a clever, brainy Scot,
And we like him quite a lot,
We all know that good old Hughie is
his name.

2
How he thrilled us with his pranks
In Newcastle's forward ranks,
And his football was the talk of all the land
Though they keep us in the dark,
Why he left St. James' Park,
'Tis a thing we really cannot understand.

3
He is nimble, he is neat,
Has a pair of tricky feet,
And a style that really is a treat to watch,
He is quick upon the grass,
Never wastes a single pass,
We all know that is because he's proper
Scotch.

4
May he always do alright,
To supporters bring delight,
May he often chance to score a winning goal
And we all wish him success
As a player we confess
Of the Chelsea team he is the life and soul.

time." Three times Hughie almost walked out. "Then," he said, "the negotiations were settled to everyone's satisfaction." He disliked the transfer system intensely and once remarked: "I have been sold like a slave for a bag of gold." This bag of gold was, by most accounts, worth £10,000, almost a new record fee, £890 short of David Jack's transfer when he moved from Bolton to Arsenal a year earlier. Although the exact sum was again a closely guarded secret, some reports claimed that the amount for Gallacher's signature was as high as £12,000, a figure which was never denied by Chelsea or Newcastle.

When the news hit Tyneside the following day, everyone was amazed. After netting 143 goals in only 174 games for United, how the club's most prolific goalscorer was ever despatched against his will incensed fans everywhere. Critics had a field day. The *Newcastle Daily Journal* noted, 'Newcastle are bound to miss him, for he is the best centre-forward of the day'.

So why did United let him go? It was said that certain club officials were fed up with his prima donna antics, his drinking and night-life habits. The level of Hughie's drinking was undoubtedly exaggerated and it had never affected his football — the goals kept coming. It was even said that it was Hughie's pleasure to take a pint or two before the match, at the Strawberry Inn just outside St James' Park, and once United's trainer had to be sent to fetch the centre-forward when he was late for changing. True or not, his reputation affected his relationship with Newcastle's directors. They had put up with enough and were ready to cash-in when they could.

There were also stories of dressing-room division during the previous season. Gallacher was blamed for most of it, although teammate George Mathison said categorically that he had a great relationship with most of the players. The United half-back, even 50 years later, still had no idea why Newcastle United let Gallacher go. "It was a perplexing question to

many. We missed his goals for quite a while," he said.

The day Gallacher left Tyneside, United boss Andy Cunningham, gave him a remarkable public send-off. Hughie was reported as saying: "I did well at Airdrie. I have done well at Newcastle. I'll do well anywhere." However, he never quite matched his game by game form or popularity anywhere else.

Chelsea's manager, David Calderhead, was a happy man. He said: "We have been wanting Hugh Gallacher for a long time." Prior to 1930-31 Chelsea had been languishing in the Second Division with little likelihood of enticing Gallacher. Now they had gained promotion and managed to capture his signature. Newcastle United missed Gallacher all right. His successors, Scots Duncan Hutchison and Duncan Lindsay, hardly endeared themselves to Tyneside's public.

From industrial Lanarkshire and a Tyneside in the midst of depression, 27-year-old Gallacher found himself in the relatively properous south — the capital and a rich society. Gone were the pits and smokey skies of Scotland and the North-East. He found himself in the very heart of London, in digs at fashionable Barons Court. Hughie was wary of his move to the metropolis. He was a stranger, a northerner at that, in a big city with a notoriously cold heart. He had never been comfortable about the south, but soon familiar voices welcomed the new recruit to the capital.

Chelsea, at that time, had a large Scots influence. Boss Calderhead had been 23 years at the helm. He was a former Scotland international and never concealed his liking for the intricate skills associated with players from over the border. He was a man of action and few words. 'The Chelsea Sphinx' they called him and he brought plenty of his own countrymen to Stamford Bridge. It was a Scots haven, perfectly suited for Gallacher.

Former Scotland centre-forward,

A welcome to Stamford Bridge by a Chelsea official.

Andy Wilson, had been at Chelsea for seven happy years. Scots fullback Tommy Law was there too, a Wembley Wizard like Gallacher. He was soon joined by another of that side when Calderhead splashed more money out before the season started, bringing Huddersfield's Alec Jackson to London for £8,500. Another international from the north also joined the growing tartan

Andy Wilson (top) and Tommy Law, two Scots internationals at Chelsea.

band. Six thousand pounds was spent on Alec Cheyne, the Aberdeen celebrity. Gallacher had played a part in signing both Jackson and Cheyne, who had been friends of his for years. Also on the Chelsea staff were two Geordies — winger Jackie Crawford and George Pearson. In fact there was hardly a Londoner in sight.

Gallacher, Chelsea's expensive new centre-forward.

Chelsea were determined to gain a top placing in Division One. For six seasons they had attempted to gain promotion from Second Division obscurity. They had been close on three occasions in the 1920s but at last, in 1930, they were successful, runners-up to champions Blackpool. A new era had begun at Stamford Bridge. On paper anyway, their star-studded line-up was one of the best in Britain and huge crowds flocked to south-west London. It was in 1930 that the now-famous Shed was built and the attendance averaged almost 42,000 in the season, with over 75,000 for a tussle with Arsenal, creating a record crowd.

Chelsea started the 1930-31 season with two away fixtures. Hughie Gallacher's debut for his new club was at Grimsby Town on 30 August. Chelsea won 1-0, through a Tommy Law penalty. Three days later his second game meant, ironically, a return to St James' Park. What a reception awaited the former Newcastle star. A huge attendance gathered for the late-afternoon kick-off. The largest-ever midweek crowd anywhere converged on St James' Park — 68,386 turned up. It was a new record gate for United, one that still stands, and an estimated 10,000 more were locked out. Hundreds sat precariously on the stand roof, others braved tree-top perches along Leazes Terrace. The two teams on that 3 September afternoon were:

> **United:** McInroy; Nelson, Fairhurst, Mathison, Hill, Naylor, Cape, Starling, Lindsay, McDonald, Wilkinson.
> **Chelsea:** Millington; Smith, Law, Russell, Townrow, Bishop, Crawford, Cheyne, Gallacher, Miller, Pearson.

Chelsea had injury problems and much was expected of Gallacher, skipper on his return. He was up against his former sparring partner, Jack Hill, once more. They were to have a real captain's tussle, but thankfully no major off-the-ball incidents occurred.

Gallacher was greeted with a 'storm of cheering' never witnessed before or since for a visiting player. Cloth caps waved and how the Geordies cheered. The hero-worship was still there, despite a change in colours. Gallacher admitted in later years that the demonstration of sheer adulation from the Newcastle fans had been the most memorable moment of his life.

Twice before half-time the former United centre-forward went close for his new club, but Albert McInroy saved well. Gallacher was, in fact, a little eager and was often caught in the Magpies' offside trap. As usual, he protested at decisions fervently. Newcastle full-back Jimmy Nelson was carried off after the break, an incident that served only to spur on the home side. Deadlock was broken

when Jonathan Wilkinson, Gallacher's deputy for most of the previous season, lobbed the ball to the far post where winger Jackie Cape rushed in to head home the winning goal.

Hughie's first appearance in front of the Stamford Bridge fans was against Manchester United the following weekend. Over 55,000 saw Chelsea win 6-2 and Gallacher impressed with a scintillating display. He scored twice and helped Alec Cheyne to grab a hat-trick, also on his home debut. Expectation was high for the season ahead. However, this bright start was not continued and in the opening weeks of the season results were disappointing, with only two wins in the first eight games. Worse was to follow. They lost

6-2 to Birmingham, 5-1 to rivals Arsenal at Stamford Bridge and 6-2 again, this time at the hands of Derby County.

All this was despite Chelsea fielding a team of quality players, stars galore. They had dazzling individualism, but were unimpressive with team play and pattern. They found it difficult to provide the blend that such a collection of soccer talent should have been able to display. Chelsea possessed no fewer than ten internationals. In goal was Sam Millington, safe and reliable. He was first-choice at Stamford Bridge for six seasons. George Smith partnered Glaswegian Tommy Law at full-back. Smith, a veteran with Chelsea, was nearing the end of his career and left-back Law, who was to spend his entire professional career with the Londoners, went on to win two caps. Law possessed a most famous tackle and he was also Gallacher's great friend and 'protector' when in London.

Chelsea's half-back line was as strong as it could be. Sam Irving played for Ireland on 18 occasions and won an FA Cup medal with Cardiff in 1927. Londoner Jack Townrow was an England international centre-half. An England colleague of Townrow's was Sid Bishop, another Londoner. Formerly captain of West Ham, he arrived at Chelsea from Leicester City in 1926. Also to play in those midfield positions was Harold Miller, yet another international who turned out in over 360 games for the Blues over 15 seasons.

The forward line was exceptional, all internationals and all able to score goals. Alec Jackson and Jackie Crawford held the wing positions. Jackson, known at the 'Gay Cavalier', was almost as well-known as Gallacher. He had won Cup and Championship medals with Huddersfield Town's formidable sides and was a regular in Scotland's line-up, winning 17 caps all told, including the Wizard's match when he netted a hat-trick. Jackson possessed a happy

Chelsea v Manchester City at Stamford Bridge. Gallacher sends a header towards goal.

knack of scoring, was fast, brainy and unorthodox. Crawford came from Tyneside, a Jarrow product, and spent a decade with Chelsea. Only 5ft 2in, he switched wings to accommodate Jackson and went on to play for England in 1931.

Inside-forward Andy Wilson was a true artist and a master at keeping the forward line moving with long or short passes. He was the Chelsea crowd's favourite, arriving from Middlesbrough in 1923 for £6,000, then a record fee. A former Scotland captain, he hailed from Lanarkshire like Gallacher, and amazingly overcame the handicap of a shattered left arm, a wartime injury sustained in 1918. Gallacher's other partner up front was another Glaswegian, Alec Cheyne. Like Wilson, he had subtle ability and grace on the ball. He made

his name with Aberdeen and was the master of the in-swinging corner-kick.

It was quite a combination of talent. Chelsea's star line-up had their moments when patterns did knit together. They sent Sunderland heading back north with a 5-0 thrashing, Gallacher scoring two goals, while Grimsby Town also received the treatment, going down by the same scoreline. In that match with the Mariners, Hughie Gallacher found himself in deep trouble once more. He was still on the receiving end of some rough handling by opposing defenders and, on this occasion, failed to restrain his temper. After the little Scot had been badly fouled, he retaliated and used abusive and foul language at the referee. He was sent off and was suspended for another long period, missing much of

January's and February's fixtures. Gallacher later said of the incident: "Once again my hasty tongue had got me into trouble."

Yet, as it turned out, the two-month suspension coincided with a bad injury — the first of only a handful in his career. Gallacher broke a bone in his foot and had to rest up anyway. However, there was a sting in the tail. Being suspended, Hughie again received no wages. Off he went, back to Bellshill, to find home comforts and an income of sorts from other activities.

Hughie returned to the Chelsea side against Blackburn Rovers in March and marked his comeback with a goal in a 3-2 win. The Londoners' fortunes for the rest of the season were mixed.

70

Inconsistency persisted and they finished the season in mid-table, 12th, a long way behind champions Arsenal. Gallacher was top scorer for his club once more, but with a relatively poor individual total of 14 goals in 31 outings.

Gallacher's first season with Chelsea was, in his own words, "none too happy." The season ended with

Gallacher and Andy Wilson discuss the centre-forward's latest suspension.

Gallacher (centre) goes close against Everton.

Chelsea's new Scottish import asking for a transfer. He could not settle and longed for his 'second home', the North-East. Gateshead, one of the country's poorest clubs, made a bold approach for his services during the year, while one of the League's richest outfits, Arsenal, were also said to be interested. Chelsea, however, would not even discuss a move with the Scot. His request was lodged in the wastepaper basket and he was told that he would be staying at Stamford Bridge for a long time yet.

On the international front, Gallacher, like all other Scots playing in the Football League, was out in the cold. Following the outcry surrounding his decision a year earlier, to play for Newcastle rather than Scotland, the Football League had placed a ban on its players being released to any country other than England. This hampered the progress

Scotland missed Gallacher's goals in International football.

of the other Home nations. The Scottish FA resolved not to pick any Anglo-Scot; it was Home-Scots from now on. The decision was certainly a gallant one, considering the amount of Scottish talent that now played south of the border. Scotland tried several centre-forwards in Gallacher's shirt over the next few years: Battles, Yorston, McGrory and Easson. More Scottish League centre-forwards came in, including Boyd, Dewar and McFadyen. However, most failed, and none ever matched the Gallacher record in the national blue jersey. The Scots missed his immense skills and his flair to produce his best on the big occasion. He possessed unflagging aggression as he held the line and his runs at defences were capable of bringing gasps of amazement from fans and fellow players alike. Journalist Ivan Sharpe said of the Scot: "I have seen no centre-forward to equal Gallacher."

The London toff pictured at Stamford Bridge with fashionable fedora headware and cigarette.

Gallacher scores for Chelsea against Sheffield United.

CHAPTER NINE

TROUBLE AND STRIFE AT THE BRIDGE

"I believe a footballer should be paid like all artists, according to his drawing power."
Hughie Gallacher

OVER the next two years, Hughie Gallacher experienced a varied life, becoming one of London's toffs and a regular frequenter of the capital's nightlife. He had brushes with the law, accepted illegal payments and was at the centre of a summer of discontent at Stamford Bridge that shook the club. On the football field, he just missed a trip to Wembley in the FA Cup Final.

He was appointed Chelsea captain for the opening of the 1931-2 season, but injury and team changes never gave his side a settled line-up and results were again indecisive. By Christmas, Chelsea had slipped to next-to-bottom of the table. Wilson,

Irving and Townrow, all experienced and noted players, ended their careers during the season and appeared in few games. Altogether, 26 different names turned out for Chelsea that campaign, an indication of their problems. Despite League difficulties, Chelsea set off on an FA Cup run in January 1932, with a game at lowly Tranmere Rovers on Merseyside.

It was Gallacher who saved the Londoners at that first hurdle. They were a goal down at Prenton Park before Hughie netted twice and in

Chelsea 1931-2. Back row (left to right): Carter, Barber, Millington, Miller, Bishop, Pearson. Front: Jackson, Gallacher, Oakton, Rankin, Crawford, Weaver.

the end Chelsea earned a replay. He scored again in a highly entertaining 5-3 victory which took the Blues to a London derby with fellow Division One side, West Ham United, at Stamford Bridge. A crowd of 36,657 saw the match and another

WITH CHE

WITH THE BANK OF ENGLAND AND

THATS ELEVEN HUGHIE!

HOCH MON! I'M ONLY PRACTISING

Bert Wright

HUGHIE GALLACHER.

ALEC JACKS AND HIS £10.000 Sm

Gallacher goal as the Hammers were beaten 3-1. In the fifth round, Chelsea faced Sheffield Wednesday, then riding high alongside Arsenal and Everton at the top of the table. Gallacher missed the tie through injury, but Chelsea eventually went through after a Hillsborough replay in front of a 60,004 crowd to earn a quarter-final meeting with Liverpool.

Gallacher returned to face one of his sternest markers, 'Tiny' Bradshaw, the Liverpool pivot. A rival he may have been, but he was also one of Hughie's pals, a fellow Wembley Wizard and someone who

(bottom, centre): Chelsea's visit to Tranmere Rovers was a big attraction for the Merseyside club. The game was dubbed the visit of 'the Bank of England and Scotland'.

(below): Gallacher, in the unusual Chelsea stripes scores his club's second goal against Tranmere, rounding 'keeper Gray.

Chelsea v Liverpool at Anfield. Another goal for Gallacher, tapping the ball into the net with Elisha Scott looking on.

AT HOYLAKE—*By Bert Wright.*

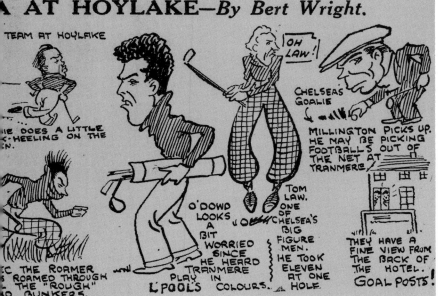

Tiny Bradshaw, 6ft 2in and over 13st, faced Gallacher in the Cup meeting with Liverpool.

knew Lanarkshire well. Bradshaw possessed a massive build at almost 6ft 2in and he and Gallacher battled it out all afternoon at Anfield. Another big crowd, over 57,000, saw Chelsea's stars play to their true form and return south victorious with a 2-0 success. 'Geordie' Pearson scored, along with Gallacher, a simple tap-in from a fierce Miller shot that Liverpool's goalkeeper, Elisha Scott, could not hold. It was

Hughie's fifth Cup goal in four games.

The clubs in the hat for the semi-final draw were Chelsea, Manchester City, Arsenal — at the height of their 1930s mastery — and Gallacher's former club, Newcastle United. And fate saw that Chelsea came out with the Tynesiders. It was Chelsea's third appearance in an FA Cup semi-final and one of the previous games had been against Newcastle United, in 1911. Chelsea had never won the FA Cup and after the semi-final at Leeds Road, Huddersfield, they were not to do so on this occasion either.

Within 25 minutes, Newcastle were 2-0 ahead through Jack Allen, Gallacher's eventual replacement at St James' Park, and Tommy Lang, whose goal was brilliantly made by Hughie's friend Jimmy Boyd.

Chelsea rallied, spurred on by Gallacher who always raised his game against the Magpies. Before half-time, a mistake by Newcastle's Roddie McKenzie let in Gallacher. He darted forward and in a flash the ball was in the net. Chelsea had a chance but, despite periods of intense pressure, they could not get the ball past England goalkeeper Albert McInroy. Hughie said afterwards: "He was in wonder form and when we forced corner after corner in the closing minutes only he prevented the equalizer." Chelsea went out with honour — they had lost to the eventual Cup-winners. It was the closest Gallacher ever came to an FA Cup medal.

As in almost every season to date, individually it had been a good year for the Scot. Chelsea recovered League form, finishing 12th for the

second season running, and Hughie found the net on 30 occasions, his best record in London. Near the end of the season he took his revenge on Newcastle United, claiming a hat-trick for Chelsea in a 4-1 drubbing of the Geordies at Stamford Bridge.

Some of his goals in that season were exceptional. Against West Ham he had been almost marked out of the game by the big and burly Jim Barrett and was receiving some crude attention from West Ham players and fans alike. Gallacher never hid and was always liable to produce the unexpected. Chelsea forced a corner. Gallacher looked up only to see the enormous frame of 14-stone Barrett blocking his view. But this time he waited for the cross, fell back, allowed the centre-half's headed clearance to fall to him and volleyed a truly fabulous cross-shot into the top of the net. It was typical of the man's intelligent play, quick thinking and control of the ball.

On the field events went well. Off the pitch, however, it was not the same story. During September and after a night on the town, Hughie found himself up against a shouting and taunting mob out to bait him. Gallacher had been to the cinema — harmless entertainment — but had then got caught up in an argument with jeering Fulham fans in a cafe in Walham Green. Events turned ugly, fists flew and the police were called. Gallacher, nursing a black eye, was arrested for disorderly conduct. He was bailed from gaol and the following morning appeared at West London Police Court. The authorities did not convict the Scottish international, but he was ordered to put ten shillings into the poor-box. Despite the lenient sentence the London Press had a field day. The story, grossly exaggerated, was blazoned all over the country, to Gallacher's disgust. Chelsea did not like his conduct or explanation and dropped him from the weekend's League visit to St James' Park, Newcastle, a trip

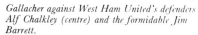

Gallacher against West Ham United's defenders Alf Chalkley (centre) and the formidable Jim Barrett.

Gallacher was looking forward to immensely. Hughie was furious with both the Press and the club. He had been unjustly treated by his reckoning, the incident being blown out of proportion, and he was later to say how the matter affected his relationship with Chelsea's management: "I think that started our break-up."

That was one example of how Gallacher, with his star image, could do nothing without the ever-watching newspapers plastering his name over the back pages. Tales of his undoing were frequent. They branded him a trouble-maker, even a drunk, and it was most hurtful to the man. He liked a tipple or two, but who does not? Gallacher admitted: "I was fond of a drink." But he was never a drunk or a trouble-maker. Deep down, he was a soft-spoken individual, most clashes being caused by people giving him a constant supply of free drink and by others keen to rile the infamous Gallacher temper.

Jack Bowers, the Derby and England forward, and later a colleague of Gallacher's at the Baseball Ground, spoke of Gallacher on one of his trips to play Chelsea in the capital. He said that on a sightseeing trip he came across a crowd of people just after the pubs had closed. He stopped to see what was going on and saw a chap lying flat on the pavement. It was Gallacher, after being in trouble and in quite a mess. Bowers and his colleagues were quite pleased in a way, for they were playing Chelsea the next day and thought that would keep Gallacher quiet for the game. In fact, he was absolutely brilliant and scored the winning goal in Chelsea's 2-1 victory. Bowers said: "I couldn't believe my eyes when I saw him on that pitch after what we had seen the night before."

Dick Spence, another England player who was at Stamford Bridge during Gallacher's time there, remembers the centre-forward as a most warm-hearted and kind man,

A personal letter to Hughie from Vivian Woodward, the former England, Tottenham and Chelsea amateur star.

Brighton v Chelsea. Gallacher challenges the home goalkeeper during an FA Cup tie.

Hughie (right) pictured with friends.

The London Evening News' *cartoonist, Harold Gittins, captures the Chelsea v Arsenal meeting at Highbury in 1932. Gallacher and Alex James are the focus of attention.*

but who had a problem with drink. However, as Spence also confirmed: "I never knew it to affect his performance on the field." The chief cause, though, of most of Gallacher's problems in the capital, and for that matter the rest of his life, were the dozens of hangers-on and phoneys that congregated around the star wherever he went. Hughie just could not cope with them. They offered him alcohol and entertainment and he could not say no. The company he sometimes kept in London as a Chelsea player did him nothing but harm.

Among some of his so-called friends were people who also gave Gallacher the opportunity of accepting illegal payments. He was given a reputation and in those years there were several stories of Hughie arranging himself additional money to boost his earnings. Some called them bribes; they were never that, for Gallacher would never 'fix' a match. The financial make up of football, however, was a major irritation to the Scot. He disliked

the system to its core. Gallacher was a bit of a rebel when it came to wages and football — and he had a point.

One feature article written many years later had Gallacher bracketed with Hollywood actor, Clark Gable, in the stardom stakes. However, there was a mammoth difference between the two — money. Gable earned thousands of dollars a week, while Hughie picked up a fraction of that during his career, a wage packet of between £7 and £8 per week, dropping to £6 in the summer months. If he was selected for his country he would get an extra £6 a game, and a £60 signing-on fee as part of any transfer. There was a huge disparity and Gallacher was aggrieved.

He always maintained that he should be paid more. In a 1934 article he wrote: 'To a poor man the wages received by a first-class footballer are not low. But I believe a footballer should be paid like all artists, according to his drawing power.' He resented what other sportsmen could earn in the 1920s and 1930s. Tennis stars like Fred Perry, or Frenchmen Borotra and Lacoste received thousands. Golfers had very good salaries and boxers, including his acquaintance, Tommy Milligan, were given heavy purses for a fight. In the USA, baseball stars were getting the equivalent of £10,000 a year, while English cricketers were on more money than top footballers. England's best batsmen and bowlers, such as Hobbs, Sutcliffe and Hammond, received £10-15 per match. Even in football, managers could get sizeable earnings. Herbert Chapman, of Huddersfield and Arsenal, and Peter McWilliam, of Middlesbrough and Spurs, were reportedly earning as much as £2,000 a year. Yet the nation's star footballers were restricted to around £500 a year. It was a poor man's sport.

With this in mind, Hughie would bend the rules and he was not alone. After he stopped playing he admitted: "Knowing the ropes I also picked up a bit of cash from other quarters." In 1950 he recorded one of those incidents which revolved around a Chelsea-Forest FA Cup

meeting. The club's directors turned down a player's approach for an additional win bonus which did not go down well in the dressing-room. But there was always money available from 'other quarters', as Hughie said. He was approached by a wealthy mill-owner: 'If you win today, there's a 'pony' waiting as a personal gift for you'. A pony, being £25, was a welcome boost and three times the weekly wage. Chelsea won 3-1, Gallacher netted two goals and that week he earned £40 all told, his unofficial gift supplementing the legal wage and win bonus.

Gallacher would always have an ear for that type of additional revenue. He would not, however, become involved in bribes, which were frequently on offer too. In 1924, during the early part of his career at Airdrie, he was approached by a couple of strangers who offered him £75 — big money then — to take it easy in a forthcoming Cup tie against Ayr United. Gallacher immediately said: "No thanks." The offer was raised to £100 but the answer was the same. In fact, this sort of illegal payment incensed the man to try even harder. Against Ayr, Gallacher netted the winner.

Money was the focus of a player revolt at Stamford Bridge in 1932. Top Chelsea stars, including Gallacher, together with some names from across London at Arsenal, had been approached by Continental clubs with unrestricted wage rules. Attractive salaries were offered and several players were tempted. They tried to obtain more cash from their clubs as a result. The star footballers reckoned they were worth more money than ordinary players and major disagreements with Chelsea officials followed. It was indeed a summer of discontent at Chelsea that had the consequence of an almost total break-up.

Player-power was rife, while discipline at Chelsea was never good. When Gallacher was appointed skipper he commented that it was a position with 'very little power'. The Blues' management was weak with so many temperamental big names around. They clashed

over money, over training, at their off-the-field activities and also over Players' Union membership, then not a popular organization with the establishment.

Alec Jackson, one of Gallacher's best friends, fell out with the club and was placed on the transfer list. He wanted more than the maximum wage and put up a bold stand. He lost and was virtually forced out of League football at 26 years of age, a great loss to the game. Eventually Jackson played non-League soccer and later went to France. Gallacher agreed whole-heartedly with the winger's stand over money. Chelsea were adamant, though. They were going to tighten discipline. It was said that they did not care if they lost Jackson, Gallacher, Cheyne or Law — or any of their big names. Principle came first.

Once Jackson had been forced out, Gallacher thought long and hard about staying at Stamford Bridge, as did other colleagues. He had been approached by Sunderland earlier in the season but it was nothing to the offers that came from the Continent. French club, Nimes, met both Gallacher and Tommy Law in a London hotel. The Scots asked for a massive package of a £3,000 signing-on fee, £20 per week and a three-year contract each. Without much hesitation the French officials agreed. In time, though, the deal fell through, although two other Chelsea stars, Andy Wilson and Alec Cheyne, left for France, admittedly for a reduced deal.

Both Law and Gallacher re-signed for Chelsea but the scars of three bitter months remained. New faces arrived. Another Scottish international — and one from Lanarkshire too — headed south when Rangers full-back Bob Macauley, was purchased. Alan Craig, also from Gallacher-country near Bellshill, was another to be capped by the Scots. But again it proved to be a season of frustration and disappointment for Chelsea fans. The star names sounded good, but they achieved little on the field. The 1932-3 season showed that success could not be bought, a harsh reminder that the purchase of expensive international talent is no guarantee of triumph.

Chelsea struggled all season. They finished in 18th position, only two points away from doomed clubs Bolton Wanderers and Blackpool, with a relegation dog-fight between Chelsea, Leicester City and Wolves, who all ended on the same points. Three results saved Chelsea's hide. First, in April they met Leeds United at the Bridge and won 6-0 with every forward scoring. It was Chelsea's biggest First Division victory up to then. They followed that with a 4-1 success over fellow strugglers Leicester City and then secured crucial points in a visit to Maine Road. Manchester City had just lost to Everton in the FA Cup Final and were suffering a post-Wembley hangover. Gallacher cashed in, netting a hat-trick in a dazzling display, one of his best for the Londoners. They won 4-1 and had cheated the drop to the Second Division.

In those three games, Hughie netted five vital goals. It had been another good season for him. After starting fresh as ever — he grabbed six goals in three games — he went on to score 19 goals all told and topped the side's scoring chart. For the tenth consecutive time he was his club's top scorer — a consistent performance without a doubt.

Alec Jackson. One of the best wingers around during the inter-war years.

CHAPTER TEN

PARTING OF THE WAYS

"I don't like London. I can't get used to the climate."

Hughie Gallacher

CHELSEA appointed a new manager for the start of the 1933-4 season. Dave Calderhead retired, after a marathon spell in charge of the Blues, and former Huddersfield Town, Arsenal and latterly Birmingham boss, Leslie Knighton, took control of the Pensioners. He had also been in charge of Manchester City and had a wealth of experience behind him in order to establish an effective unit from the considerable talent still at Stamford Bridge.

As in previous years, more Scottish blood arrived in London to join Chelsea's tartan clan. International goalkeeper John Jackson, signed from Partick Thistle, joined Gallacher at the Bridge. It was a strange transfer as he had to compete with Chelsea's England goalkeeper, Vic Woodley, the latter usually getting the nod. Jackson, though, was the seventh Scottish international to be at Chelsea during the time Gallacher was there.

Injury and poor form disrupted the new manager's revival plan. Gallacher missed six games early in the season and Chelsea again

John Jackson, who arrived to complement the Scots contingent at Stamford Bridge.

struggled. They occupied bottom place for almost seven months with only three victories in 20 games before Christmas. When relegation appeared a certainty, incredibly a rally took place, starting with a double Easter victory over Portsmouth. Five matches brought ten points — all without Hughie Gallacher at centre-forward. He missed much of March and April — out of the relegation battles with Sheffield United, Birmingham and Newcastle United — through another lengthy suspension. He was brought before an FA disciplinary hearing because of more on-the-field antics and severely punished.

Chelsea steered clear of the drop by two points, while Gallacher's old club, Newcastle United, together with Sheffield United, faced Second Division football the following August. The Scot played 28 games that season, the lowest turn-out for Gallacher in English football. Yet he still managed to become Chelsea's top goal poacher, as ever, with 16 goals — a marvellous ratio of goals per game.

Despite FA suspension, Hughie

Gallacher in action, as usual in the thick of things with the opposition goalkeeper.

was back in football in time to be recalled to the Scotland team for the battle with England at Wembley at the end of the season. It had been a four-year absence for Gallacher from the Scottish XI, with selectors again choosing England-based players. A crowd of 92,693, a record attendance for a Wembley international, saw a convincing English victory. The Scots went down 3-0, only the second time in 19 internationals that Hughie Gallacher had tasted defeat. Now past 30 years of age, he could still impress the critics. Hughie was at the focus of a Scots revival. It was noted: 'Thirty minutes of the second half was definitely Scotland's, and who could forget the insistence of Gallacher'.

On this occasion Ernest Hart, the Leeds United centre-half, found himself chasing shadows as Gallacher moved freely across the field — the ideal roving centre-forward years ahead of his time — turning up on both wings as often as he was seen in the centre-forward position. Chelsea teammate, 'Jakey' Jackson was between the posts for the Scots, having been called up from Chelsea Reserves.

The season had been a difficult one for Gallacher at Chelsea. His relationship with the new manager was not ideal and there was much transfer talk. The Scot was keen to try pastures new. During the closing months of 1933, a swap deal involving Sunderland's Bobby Gurney was rumoured. Hughie said: "How I longed for it to be true." A return to the North-East would have been perfect for Gallacher but

nothing came of the proposed transfer. He pressed for a move and it was reported that Everton were interested, to replace the injured Dixie Dean. Both clubs agreed terms, but again, the deal fell through. Manchester United were also linked, as were Gateshead

Gallacher in full flight . . . en route to goal once more.

again. But come the summer, Gallacher remained at Stamford Bridge. However, his days on the Chelsea staff were numbered. After much transfer speculation during his stay alongside the Thames, a deal was soon to be completed.

Following a mini-tour to Germany, where Gallacher saw Hitler's recently-installed Nazi regime at first hand and had to give the Nazi salute prior to a game, he did not figure in the starting line-up for Chelsea's opening games of the 1934-5 season. The place he had held for the last four years was handed to George Mills, for much of the time Gallacher's deputy. Only a handful of appearances followed before his last match for the Pensioners, on 3 November against Leeds United. Despite all the moments of controversy and dispute in London, Gallacher had enjoyed most of his stay in the capital but now it was time for a move. He left behind many memories, most of all games against Arsenal — winners of five League Championships and FA Cup Finalists three times during the 1930s — the team of the era.

They fielded Hughie's ally, Alex James, along with names like Bastin, Jack, Hapgood, Drake and Hulme to name but a few of an awesome team. Gallacher relished facing the Gunners as much as turning out against Newcastle United and those games produced a special atmosphere with attendances rarely less than 60,000 and usually topping 70,000. Hughie, as always, revelled in the big occasion and netted five goals in nine games. Arsenal came out on top, Chelsea winning only two of the meetings, but Gallacher proved he was one of the best.

Chelsea, with Gallacher as skipper, were invited to be the opponents when Arsenal's new West Stand was opened in 1932 in the presence of the Prince of Wales, later King Edward VIII. It was a special occasion, for apart from FA Cup Finals, royalty rarely attend

football games in Britain and Hughie was the centre of attraction as ever. As captain he introduced his Chelsea team to the Prince before the kick-off and gave his special guest a sweeping bow. Then, in a sudden rush of enthusiasm, he confounded everyone when he placed a friendly arm around the future monarch's waist as he walked along the line. Cameras clicked and the papers loved it. Criticized in some quarters for his less than respectful pose, it was typical Gallacher. No matter what he did he would make headlines.

Meetings with Arsenal also brought the stocky centre-forward into contest with the Gunners' formidable pivot, tall and powerful Herbie Roberts. In front of the usual capacity crowd, a sparring match would take place that had fans from both camps enthralled. Gallacher took a customary battering but he always gave as good as he got. One such encounter saw Roberts having the better of the tussle, not least through his sheer physical domin-

Chelsea v Arsenal. Gallacher challenges Frank Moss with Herbie Roberts in attention.

Hughie Gallacher, with his arm around the Prince of Wales, introducing the Chelsea team before the match against Arsenal to mark the opening of Highbury's new stand.

ation of Gallacher. Then Chelsea won a corner and as the ball was cleared, a red-shirted figure was seen lying prostrate on the pitch. It was Arsenal's England centre-half. Few had seen what had occurred, but Tom Whittaker, then the Highbury club's trainer, dashed on and was seen sponging Roberts' face. Gallacher had dished out his own retribution with a classic right-hook, drawn from his days in the Hamilton gym.

On the field Hughie could be a touch nasty, but most players agreed that his bark was always worse than his bite. He would help youngsters, even in opposition ranks too, and had his soft moments. On a Chelsea visit to Sunderland, Alec Hastings, a future Scotland wing-half, noted his first meeting with Hughie. Hastings was only 18 years old and marking Gallacher. He said: "I never hated anyone so much." From the kick-off, Gallacher snarled, baited and taunted the youngster throughout the game. But after the final whistle, Hughie went to the Sunderland dressing-room and held out his hand to the raw Hastings, saying: "Good luck to you, son. You can take it. I'm sorry I needled you."

Before Gallacher's departure from Stamford Bridge he went through a disturbing time off the field, firstly with divorce proceedings and then more drama in a bankruptcy court. For years Hughie had attempted to seek a divorce from his first wife. He lost a first action in 1926, failed with an appeal in 1927 but won a third case in 1932. Then another appeal followed, which he won. The outcome of the long and drawn out procedure was that the international star ended up without a penny. In October 1934 his financial situation was spelt out in court, and, of course, in the Press. He had debts of £787, a colossal sum in the 1930s. Gallacher attributed his insolvency to liability of the divorce costs and both the bankruptcy court and the Press treated the Scot fairly and were sympathetic. It was noted: 'The enormous bill for costs was overwhelming and it was no fault of Mr Gallacher's'.

The month before, Gallacher also

had another appointment, this time of a happier nature. He was married to his long time girlfriend, Hannah Anderson. They tried to keep their wedding a quiet affair but that proved impossible. Crowds and cameras, including the newsreel of the day, flocked to Hammersmith Registry Office to see the couple wed — and a few hours later he was playing for Chelsea.

In Gallacher's four and a half years at Stamford Bridge, Chelsea won no cups or titles; in fact they had struggled for most of the time. But his tally of 81 goals in 144 games was an impressive statistic and he was the club's top goalscorer in four successive seasons. No one in the country could better his consistency. Approaching 32 years of age, Hughie thought he still had a few years in him yet and so did Derby County boss, George Jobey.

Jobey came to London hoping to sign an Arsenal player but when the deal fell through, Gallacher's name was suggested to him. It was Alex James who arrived at Hughie's flat in Kensington to tell him of Derby County's search for a centre-forward. James knew Gallacher wanted a move north desperately and, just as

Gallacher and Jackson (right) in a goalmouth scramble. Note how Gallacher, at 5ft 5in, gets the highest.

Leicester City's goalkeeper beats Hughie to the ball this time, in a fixture at Stamford Bridge.

importantly, needed money from a transfer to pay some of his outstanding debts. The pair met and agreed terms quickly. Hughie had a lot of respect for Jobey and said of him: "One of the greatest

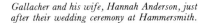

Gallacher and his wife, Hannah Anderson, just after their wedding ceremony at Hammersmith.

managers I knew." Part of the deal included a £200 fee paid directly to the Carey Street Bankruptcy Court and shortly afterwards Gallacher's debts were discharged. It was also later claimed that Derby gave Hughie a £300 gift for signing in lieu of lost benefit at Chelsea. The claim was never substantiated but several years later, Derby County and Jobey had to face an FA Commission and came under severe investigation regarding transfers and illegal payments. The manager was suspended *sine die* as a result. Hughie Gallacher was called to explain his dealings with the Rams but refused to attend the investigation. It explained, perhaps, how Jobey had managed to bring so many international stars to the Baseball Ground in the 1930s.

Jobey and Derby County had acquired a new centre-forward in a deal worth £2,750. Gallacher had a new club. The date was November 1934. Some quarters reported that it was a foolish move for Derby, that Gallacher was too old and past his best, temperamental and caused scandal wherever he went. It was a risk deal, but Gallacher replied in style. Hughie left London for the Midlands, saying, tongue in cheek: "I don't like London. I can't get used to the climate."

Hughie on the move again – from Stamford Bridge to the Baseball Ground.

CHAPTER ELEVEN

UNION WITH THE RAMS

"A quarter of an hour from the end he walked through the defence like the master he is, to get his fifth goal — a wonderful effort."

Derby Evening Telegraph

THROUGHOUT the 1930s, Derby County were one of England's best sides, being both strong Championship contenders and feared Cup fighters. Manager George Jobey had formed an exceptional set-up at the Baseball Ground and so different to Stamford Bridge's problems that Gallacher had continually encountered. In charge since 1925, Jobey was a Tynesider who had played predominantly for Newcastle United, Arsenal and Leicester. A shrewd character, he was a tough one and a highly-respected boss.

He attracted big names to Derby and in that era the Rams boasted a host of international-class footballers. Snowy-haired full-back Tom Cooper and centre-half Jack Barker were England defenders and Cooper was his country's captain. The formidable Barker was an ex-miner with a flair for attack and was Hughie Gallacher's choice as the best centre-half around in the 1930s. Wing-half Errington Keen was another England cap and had been with Gallacher on Newcastle United's staff as a youngster. 'Dally' Duncan and Sammy Crooks were

George Jobey, the Derby County manager who took a risk with Gallacher.

two international wingers with a habit of notching plenty of goals — 180 between them for Derby. Few were better at their role and the Duncan-Crooks partnership did much to put the Rams into the top five sides in the land at that time.

At centre-forward was Jack Bowers, three times named in the England line-up and who capitalized in great style on the chances made by others. One of the best in the game, Bowers was the First Division's leading scorer for two consecutive seasons up to 1934, before a badly injured knee sidelined him for a long period. It was Hughie Gallacher, now thinning on top,

Gallacher welcomed by his new teammates at the Baseball Ground. Left to right: Jack Barker, Peter Ramage, Freddie Jessop, Hughie Gallacher, Dally Duncan and Charlie Napier.

Tom Cooper (far left) and Sammy Crooks . . . two of Derby's international stars.

Jack Bowers. His injury brought Hughie to Derby.

who had to fill the role of a centre-forward and was at the peak of his career. Jobey was confident that, despite his age, Hughie could give Derby County good service, and that he could handle Gallacher's explosive and sometimes unmanageable character. It turned out to be a master-stroke of short-term business by the manager as Gallacher went on to have a marvellous union with the Rams. He was fixed up with a house at Littleover on the southern outskirts of the town and quickly settled in the Midlands.

Gallacher led the Derby attack for the first time against Birmingham at the Baseball Ground on 10 November 1934. Considerable interest was roused by his appearance and, on a miserable, wet afternoon, those present saw Gallacher at his best. He scored after only six minutes when Duncan provided a beautiful crossfield-pass. The centre-forward seized on to the chance like lightning and with a stinging left-foot shot, flashed the ball across Birmingham's England goalkeeper, Harry Hibbs, into the top corner of the net. Derby continued to press the Blues' defence, but found Hibbs in an unyielding mood. Gallacher had a lot of respect for the 5ft 9in custodian and was to say of the Brum goalkeeper: "Considering his size, Hibbs was a marvel."

At the end of 90 minutes the game ended all-square at 1-1. The *Derby Evening Telegraph* noted: 'Gallacher had proved a great success. His footwork was brilliant and his positioning clever and he was given a loud cheer as the players ran off the field'.

Hughie netted in his next appearance, at Portsmouth, and by

GALLACHER SCORES FIVE TIMES!

BLACKBURN DEFENCE SWEPT OFF ITS FEET

HUGHIE THE MASTER

DERBY COUNTY SCORED FIVE MORE GOALS THIS AFTERNOON—MAKING 14 IN TWO MATCHES!

THE hero of their brilliant 5—2 victory against Blackburn Rovers at Ewood was Hughie Gallacher, who scored all five goals.

It was a great occasion for Gallacher when, after 22 minutes, Stockill headed Crooks's corner-kick down for him to crash the ball past Binns. This was his 300th goal in Scottish and English League football.

A bad tackle by Udall gave the Rovers their chance to equalise. The referee awarded a penalty, and Bruton made no mistake with his kick.

Gallacher put the Rams ahead again, however, just before half-time, after a clever movement with Duncan and Crooks.

The second half opened with a shock for the County, Thompson scoring a glorious goal after getting round Collin.

Then the Rams butted twice—again through Gallacher. He completed his hat trick with a brilliant shot, and the fourth was provided by Crooks.

Hughie had not finished celebrating. A quarter of an hour from the end he "walked" through the defence, like the master he is, to get his fifth goal—a wonderful effort. Here's to Hughie !

15 December 1934. Gallacher makes the headlines again.

December had regained top form and was as good as at any period in his career. The move to Derby had rekindled his enthusiasm for the game. Gallacher scored nine goals in the space of three weeks. Derby defeated West Bromwich Albion 9-3, Hughie netting two, and then the Rams travelled to meet Blackburn Rovers and gained two more points in a 5-2 success, Gallacher claiming all five goals. Derby County fielded the following team at Ewood Park:

Blore; Udall, Collin, Nicholas, Barker, Hann, Crooks, Stockill, Gallacher, Ramage, Duncan.

Gallacher was both opportunist and individualist rolled into one. His first goal came from a Sammy Crooks corner. Stockill nodded the ball down and Gallacher crashed it into the back of the net. Just before the interval a fabulous movement between Duncan, Gallacher and Crooks ended with Hughie receiving a return pass and tapping the ball home. The two Scots, Duncan and Gallacher, combined again to give the County leader a chance and a screw-shot completed his hat-trick. Number-four came three minutes later, Gallacher reacting quickest to another teasing cross from Crooks. At this stage Derby's forwards were doing almost as they liked — Duncan and Gallacher in particular.

Some remarkable footwork by Gallacher had the Rovers defence in a desperate state. More goals had to come and Gallacher was there again. The *Derby Evening Telegraph* commented: 'A quarter of an hour from the end he walked through the defence like the master he is, to get his fifth goal — a wonderful effort'. Hughie went past Bob Pryde, the Rovers half-back, cut down the middle on his own, rounded both backs and fired past 'keeper Cliff Binns. It was the best goal of the five and capped an astonishing display.

During January and February, he also hit a purple patch, scoring in five consecutive League games with seven goals as Derby challenged

Arsenal and Sunderland for the title. They never quite made it, though, finishing the season in sixth place. Gallacher had a first-class start to his Derby career, netting 24 goals in only 30 games. Jobey's faith in the ageing star was proved faultless and needless to say Hughie was top scorer once more.

Gallacher's form saw him win another Scotland cap against England. Teaming up with his Rams colleague, Dally Duncan, Hughie was in direct contest with another teammate from the Baseball Ground, Jack Barker, who was centre-half for England. A massive attendance of 129,693, one of the

Derby pair, Gallacher and Duncan, on board the ship back to Southampton.

largest-ever in Britain, saw the meeting at Hampden Park and the big Glasgow crowd were happy enough seeing a Scotland victory. Both goals were netted by Aberdonian Duncan. It was Hughie Gallacher's last senior game for the Scots, although in the summer he was a member of the Scottish FA party that toured the USA and Canada. He and Duncan were the only two Anglos picked. It was a working holiday Hughie richly enjoyed, as he recorded, 'a trip never to be forgotten'.

The Scots team spent almost five weeks touring North America. Gallacher travelled cross-country from New York to Vancouver, stopping frequently on the trip westwards and witnessing a totally

different world of skyscrapers and totem poles. He had time to see the sights and live like a lord, as well as scoring a few goals too. Scotland won all 12 matches and Gallacher netted ten in six games, including four against Alberta FA in Calgary. The tour was well received on the other side of the Atlantic. The Scottish Football Association's official minutes record that it had been 'successful in every way'.

Gallacher's overall record for Scotland was outstanding. In 20 appearances spanning 11 years, he had netted 24 goals and, of those games, he had been on the winning side on 17 occasions. No one had scored so many goals up to then; and since, only Kenny Dalglish and Denis Law have netted more — and

in many more outings. Additionally, due to the Anglo-Scots selection problem, Hughie missed almost four years of internationals. The Wembley Wizards were undoubtedly the highlight, yet on that afternoon he did not find the net. Gallacher's five goals against Northern Ireland in 1929 remain a goalscoring record to this day.

Derby County continued playing good football in the 1935-6 season and came the closest they had to winning the Championship — and the closest for another 36 years until Brian Clough's side won the trophy in 1972. But Gallacher and company started the season in a disastrous way, losing the opening fixtures at Goodison Park 4-0 and Deepdale 1-0. The season, however, was to

develop into one of the most celebrated in the Rams' history.

Arriving at the Baseball Ground for that season were two Scots, faces Gallacher knew well. Celtic and Scotland forward Charlie Napier joined the club for £5,000 and Derby now fielded three of Scotland's five forwards that had defeated England four months earlier. Gallacher also welcomed an old pal from St James' Park, Jimmy Boyd, Newcastle United's long-serving winger, who was also capped by the Scots during the 1930s. Boyd was one of Hughie's closest friends in the game. Also to nearly sign for Jobey was none other

Jimmy Boyd who joined Gallacher at Derby.

Scotland's squad to tour America pictured outside the Waldorf Astoria Hotel in New York. The full party was: Anderson (Hearts), Cummings (Partick Thistle), Donnelly (Partick Thistle), Duncan (Derby County), Ferguson (St Johnstone), Fraser (Aberdeen), Gallacher (Derby County), Main (Glasgow Rangers), McDonald (Glasgow Rangers), Meiklejohn (Glasgow Rangers, captain), Miller (Partick Thistle), Mills (Aberdeen), Stevenson (Clyde), Smith (Kilmarnock), Walker (Hearts), Wilson (Hamilton), Wilson (Hibernian). Gallacher is sitting in the front row, fourth from the right.

than Alex James. A cash-exchange deal had been set up involving Cooper and Crooks but, when James heard that he was only being valued at £2,000, the deal fell through. Another chance of seeing both Gallacher and James in the same club side had been lost.

Among Derby's few non-international players was goalkeeper Jack Kirby, who perhaps was unlucky not to be capped because of the surfeit of brilliant 'keepers around. Jack Nicholas and Ted Udall, Tom Cooper's replacement at full-back, were two solid defenders. Peter Ramage at inside-forward was a first-class forager and foil to Gallacher up front.

After the opening set-backs against Everton and Preston, Derby embarked on a seven-game undefeated run, winning six matches to put them in the top placings of the First Division. Gallacher scored five goals in that spree and November opened with the Scotland centre-forward netting against Manchester City in a 3-0 victory, but also being sidelined with a bad shoulder injury. Derby's form slumped without the veteran's influence. They won only two of the remaining ten games up to Christmas.

Hughie was back in action for the FA Cup in January and helped the Rams on their way to the quarter-final, one step further on the road to Wembley than the previous season when they lost to Everton in the fifth round. There was, however, an almost embarrassing exit at the first hurdle against non-League Dartford. County were 2-0 down at the Baseball Ground but a late revival, initiated by Gallacher, took them to the fourth round with a 3-2 win. Hughie was not to take part in any further action, though. He was missing for another ten games, the shoulder problem proving a long and troublesome handicap to clear up.

Derby County were still in the hunt for honours in the Championship race, despite the team's inconsistency and missing Gallacher's

Gallacher and wife . . . ready for a night on the town.

skills. Perhaps a fit Gallacher would have given the Rams that 'extra boost needed to lift the title. The contest lay between Derby, Huddersfield Town, Stoke City and favourites and leaders, Sunderland. Hughie returned against West Bromwich Albion, scored two and Derby won 3-0. But to catch a very good Sunderland side, they had to perform at their best for the remainder of the season. Erratic results — a win, a draw, a win, a defeat — continued. The chance of overtaking the Wearsiders was lost by the time the two challengers met at the Baseball Ground at the end of April.

	DIVISION 1						1935-36
1	Sunderland	42	25	6	11	109:74	56
2	Derby	42	18	12	12	61:52	48
3	Huddersfield	42	18	12	12	59:56	48
4	Stoke	42	20	7	15	57:57	47
5	Brentford	42	17	12	13	81:60	46
6	Arsenal	42	15	15	12	78:48	45
7	Preston	42	18	8	16	67:64	44
8	Chelsea	42	15	13	14	65:72	43
9	Manchester C.	42	17	8	17	68:60	42
10	Portsmouth	42	17	8	17	54:67	42
11	Leeds	42	15	11	16	66:64	41
12	Birmingham	42	15	11	16	61:63	41
13	Bolton	42	14	13	15	67:76	41
14	Middlesbrough	42	15	10	17	84:70	40
15	Wolverhampton	42	15	10	17	77:76	40
16	Everton	42	13	13	16	89:89	39
17	Grimsby	42	17	5	20	65:73	39
18	West Bromwich	42	16	6	20	89:88	38
19	Liverpool	42	13	12	17	60:64	38
20	Sheffield W.	42	13	12	17	63:77	38
21	Aston Villa	42	13	9	20	81:110	35
22	Blackburn	42	12	9	21	55:96	33

The race was almost over. Sunderland were all but crowned as new Champions, yet Derby showed how close it could have been by thrashing the Roker side 4-0 and eventually finishing runners-up, eight points adrift of the Wearsiders. Gallacher scored his 16th goal of the season — and his last for the Rams. Again he was leading scorer — well ahead of Jack Bowers — fit again but not quite the same player he had been two years earlier.

Among Gallacher's goals that season was a remarkable effort against Manchester City. Hughie was a cheeky and sometimes infuriating player to oppose on the field and Frank Swift, the cheery England goalkeeper, took the brunt of Gallacher's impertinence. He was in goal for City on that afternoon at the Baseball Ground. Derby put the visitors under pressure and Swift, at almost 6ft 3in, was collecting all the crosses, with few

chances falling Gallacher's way. Hughie was getting a bit sick of this. He was to change the pattern. Then another cross came over. Swift recalled he heard a voice calling, 'Right, Frank', and Swift left the ball, thinking it was one of his defenders in a better position. In stepped Hughie Gallacher to bullet a header into the empty net, leaving Swift red-faced. Hughie turned round and said to the 'keeper: "That should teach you a lesson Frank!" Ungentlemanly you could call it. That was Hughie Gallacher. He would get up to any trick to score a goal.

Hughie was more than happy at Derby but he found himself second-choice to Bowers as the new season commenced. At 33 years of age he could not really complain, yet his goals record was still first class — 40 in 55 games for the Rams. Within himself, he reckoned, he still had two or three years and another 50 goals to score. Jobey, however, was now willing to listen to offers for the little giant of football. Gallacher could have done his job in no better way, but with Bowers fit again and Gallacher ageing, there was no place for him.

Gateshead tried to sign Hughie but failed again. Then, one morning in September 1936 — the same month that Bowers scored four goals in a 15-minute spell against Manchester United — Gallacher arrived at the Baseball Ground for training and noticed a couple of executive cars parked outside the directors' and officials' entrance. He knew something was happening. Sure enough, the cars belonged to the management of his next port of call. Within a few hours, Hughie Gallacher had been transferred to neighbouring Notts County for £2,000.

CHAPTER TWELVE

MORE BLACK 'N' WHITE

"It isn't what Hughie is doing himself, but what he is doing for the rest of the team."
Jimmy McMullan

HUGHIE Gallacher was now in the veteran class. At 33 years old, his career began the downward trek that comes to even the greatest of stars. Hughie had left a tremendous store of tales and anecdotes behind him, but there were still a few more to come in the years remaining before his boots were hung up for a final time.

Notts County officials arranged a fine house in pleasant surroundings, near Trent Bridge cricket ground, and Hughie joined the oldest club in League football, at a time when they were in the Third Division South and toiling to get back with the elite of football, under Percy Smith, the former Spurs boss. The Magpies had no fewer than seven managers during the 1930s and were going through a major upheaval. Smith needed a centre-forward to see them through a difficult spell. He had tried big names before: Arthur Chandler, over 260 goals in 12 years with Leicester, but well past his best; then Jimmy Smith, who at his peak in 1928 scored a British record 66 goals for Ayr United. Like Chandler he was not the answer and was axed

Hughie in the black and white stripes again, this time of Notts County.

early on. Hughie Gallacher was the next to be brought to Meadow Lane.

Gallacher knew that Notts County were in a bad way. Smith had spelt their problems out to the Scot, but as Gallacher recorded: "Not until I reported at their ground did I realize just how they were struggling." When he arrived for his first training session, Notts had only seven fit players to continue the new season which was some half a dozen games old. Hughie was greeted by an old pal on that morning, ex-Newcastle United reserve forward, Willie Chalmers, who was born not far from Gallacher's birthplace in Bellshill. Chalmers made Gallacher feel at home and the pair spent many an hour relaxing and chatting about their days together on Tyneside and homelands north.

Gallacher was joined by another newcomer, Irishman Con Moulson from Lincoln City, the Irish Free State's international centre-half. Bill Fallon was also a Republic of Ireland cap in the side, while a long-serving defensive partnership of Alf Feebury and Percy Mills proved a reliable duo. Percy Smith appointed Gallacher as team captain and saw his new centre-forward make an immediate impact, netting twice in his second game and soon after-wards hitting a hat-trick against Northampton Town. But the County manager did not remain in charge to see the Scot transform the side from a mid-table XI into a promotion-searching outfit. Within days, Smith was off to pastures fresh, and one of Gallacher's ex-Scotland colleagues, Jimmy McMullan, took control.

McMullan skippered the immortal Wembley Wizards back in 1928 and had strong claims to being the best Scottish half-back during those days. Small, and a marvellous playmaker for Manchester City, he had turned to management in 1933 with Oldham Athletic and then Aston Villa before heading for the Trent. Gallacher could not have been more pleased to play for his former national captain and the relationship worked superbly for Notts County.

The Magpies shot up the table and became favourites to regain Second Division status. Gallacher grabbed goals as if he were only 23 and not ten years older. It was his

first taste in the lower divisions and his finesse and experience stood out by the proverbial mile. Attendances increased dramatically as crowds packed into Meadow Lane to see Gallacher in goalscoring mood. Throughout the winter and into the opening weeks of 1937, County recorded six consecutive wins. McMullan said of Gallacher's influence on the side: "It isn't what Hughie is doing himself, but what he is doing for the rest of the team." Apart from Gallacher's goals, the side's main asset was the dressing-room spirit. They possessed a never-say-die attitude. From Christmas Day, County continued to be odds-on for promotion, heading the table and undefeated until the closing weeks of the season. One local businessman offered Gallacher £800 as a bonus if he led County into Division Two. That was a huge incentive for Hughie.

Rivals that year were Luton Town, Brighton & Hove Albion and Watford. Success seemed well in their grasp but in the final run-in, the season ended in gloom. Needing

three points from their last two games, Notts lost a crucial meeting with Brighton at Meadow Lane. County then defeated Walsall, but it was Luton who clinched the solitary promotion place, only one club from each of the north and south divisions being promoted in that era. Notts had failed narrowly and it was Hughie Gallacher's most disappointing day in football.

DIVISION 3S					1936-37	
1 Luton	42	27	4	11	103·53	58
2 Notts Co.	42	23	10	9	74·52	56
3 Brighton	42	24	5	13	74·43	53
4 Watford	42	19	11	12	85·60	49
5 Reading	42	19	11	12	76·60	49
6 Bournemouth	42	20	9	13	65·59	49
7 Northampton	42	20	6	16	85·68	46
8 Millwall	42	18	10	14	64·54	46
9 QPR	42	18	9	15	73·52	45
10 Southend	42	17	11	14	78·67	45
11 Gillingham	42	18	8	16	52·66	44
12 Clapton Orient	42	14	15	13	52·52	43
13 Swindon	42	14	11	17	75·73	39
14 Crystal Palace	42	13	12	17	62·61	38
15 Bristol R.	42	16	4	22	71·80	36
16 Bristol C.	42	15	6	21	58·70	36
17 Walsall	42	13	10	19	62·84	36
18 Cardiff	42	14	7	21	54·87	35
19 Newport	42	12	10	20	67·98	34
20 Torquay	42	11	10	21	57·80	32
21 Exeter	42	10	12	20	59·88	32
22 Aldershot	42	7	9	26	50·89	23

Notts County in 1937. Players only. Back row (left to right): Corkhill, Blyth, Moulson. Middle: Rickards, Gallacher, Chalmers, Cooper, Fallon. Front: Feebury, McLenahan, Mills.

However, his season was a personal triumph. He scored 25 goals in 33 games and this when into his 35th year. He had proved he was still fit, dangerous and able to last the pace.

Despite the side's good League form, the FA Cup in 1936-7 was a failure but it brought Gallacher a face-to-face meeting on the field with his brother-in-law, George Mathison, then skipper of Gateshead. Mathison had been at Newcastle with Gallacher and both players had married into the Anderson family. The FA Cup first-round encounter with Gateshead was one of the Scot's fondest memories. Both players were club captains — resulting in a family reunion as they tossed the coin in the centre-circle before the kick-off. Gateshead won 2-0 with Mathison scoring one of the goals from the

penalty-spot. Hughie jokingly shouted to his friend as he was about to shoot, "Miss it George — come on, miss it."

During the summer months, Gallacher was offered a contract to play for St George's FC of Malta. He turned the move down but in years to follow they persisted in approaching the striker. In fact, the Mediterranean club eventually succeeded and all was lined up for Gallacher's finale, but then war put an end to a proposed transfer.

The new 1937-8 season started well for Notts County. It was a virtual repeat of the previous campaign, but in December there was a huge blow to team spirit and the season fell apart. Jimmy McMullan, whose influence was immense, moved on to become Sheffield Wednesday's manager and

Gallacher meets brother-in-law George Mathison before the Notts County v Gateshead FA Cup tie.

(right): Hughie takes a breather in the dressing-room.

Gallacher quickly asked for a transfer. After 46 games and 32 goals for County, he was off on another change of scene, his sixth senior club, and with it a move back into the First Division. Notts County acted swiftly to replace their departing star attraction, signing Gallacher's great contemporary, Dixie Dean, another big scoop. Ageing, like Gallacher, Dean, however, never lived up to his reputation in a County shirt as had the departing Scot from Bellshill. Dixie managed only three goals during his stay at Meadow Lane.

Bradford City and Stockport County chased Gallacher, once he made it clear he no longer wanted to remain with Notts County. However, Grimsby Town were always favourite once they entered the scene. They were a First Division club and holding the reigns at Blundell Park was a former Championship-winning colleague of Hughie's from Newcastle United's 1927 team, former England centre-half Charlie Spencer. From a promotion-chasing side at Notts County, Gallacher found himself still wearing a black and white shirt, but now in the middle of a relegation scramble at Grimsby. Spencer had problems to solve with the Mariners. Injury had robbed the side of several talented players, none more important than centre-forward Pat Glover, out with a cartilage ailment on the first day of the season. The Welsh international had netted over 130 goals in the

Gallacher in black and white once more, this time with Grimsby Town.

Pat Glover, one of the most prolific goalscorers of the time.

previous four seasons and without Glover's scoring powers, the Mariners looked doomed.

Reserve leader Reg Tomlinson was tried, but he was not the answer. Spencer turned to Gallacher to rescue the side in the short term. Grimsby paid £1,000 for his signature in January 1938 and while he never totally substituted for Glover, Hughie gave the struggling side a boost and helped Grimsby steer clear of relegation, although relief did not arrive until the last day of the season.

By a strange twist, Gallacher's first appearance for Grimsby was against Newcastle United, a friendly arranged on a Cup Saturday, both clubs having an early exit that year. A crowd of 20,000 turned up at St James' Park to see the ex-Magpie star. The local Press noted: 'Probably a good half of the crowd went there more with the object of renewing acquaintance with the former Gallowgate God'. Hughie turned on an exhibition show for his still adoring Tyneside audience. He was given a tremendous reception and was moved at the warmth shown towards him. He scored and inspired Grimsby as they went 2-0 ahead, but Newcastle fought back with the eventual scoreline ending all-square at 3-3.

Gallacher found it much tougher in the competitive atmosphere of Division One. He played against Leeds United the following Wednesday, then Liverpool and West Bromwich Albion, but no goals came for Hughie. He did not find the net until his sixth game, when the Mariners defeated Huddersfield Town 4-2 during February. Goals were hard to come by in the relegation battle and Grimsby continued to find it difficult to obtain results despite having several respected names in their ranks.

Apart from Gallacher, another veteran, Jackie Bestall, was at inside-right. Skipper of the side, he was an ex-England forward and had clocked up over 400 games for Town. Harry Betmead also played for England at centre-half. Jack Hodgson was another long-serving player at full-back, while in goal was

George Tweedy, yet another England international. Signed at the same time as Gallacher were two players, Jackie Coulter, an Irish international from Everton, and Jock Beattie, an Aberdonian who

had turned out for Huddersfield, Birmingham and Wolves.

As the final week of the season arrived, six clubs — including Grimsby — were on 36 points. It was a dramatic close to the football year. Grimsby entertained Chelsea on the crucial Saturday, minus the services of Gallacher. He was left out of the clash with his former club, much to his annoyance. Back came Pat Glover and Grimsby won 2-0. That victory saved them from the Second Division by the slightest of margins. Gallacher, although pleased for the club, was not too happy about his relationship with Spencer.

At first, Gallacher enjoyed his early weeks at Blundell Park. The club were good to their players, to the extent of having a crate of beer in the dressing-room for refreshment after the match, as well giving each man a box of local fish to take home. But as soon as Hughie

Jack Hodgson (left) and Jackie Bestall, two Grimsby stalwarts.

realized that Glover would always be first choice, relationships deteriorated. He did not like sitting in the stand watching someone else leading the attack, especially when, at times, a half-fit Glover was chosen in preference to a fully-fit Gallacher. Hughie played 12 games altogether for Grimsby and dressing-room disagreements followed. Gallacher was aggrieved and made it known that he would move at the first opportunity.

His fleeting months on the Humber coast also saw the sometimes moody genius in trouble with the law. He was required to appear in court again. This time Gallacher had been picked up by police after being involved in a road accident with a cyclist and was found to be driving under the influence of alcohol. These, of course, were pre-breathalyser days, but courts were tough, even in 1938. He was banned from driving for a year and fined £12. The incident also meant that any chance of reconciliation with Grimsby officials was impossible. Another transfer was the only alternative.

Grimsby line-up in 1938 in a change strip for a match against West Bromwich Albion at The Hawthorns. Standing (left to right): Vincent, J.Shaw, Theaker, Atherton, Hodgson, Betmead. Front: Hall, H.Shaw, Gallacher, Craven, Coulter, Buck.

CHAPTER THIRTEEN

NOSTALGIC RETURN

"I have been north, south, east and the Midlands, but no place can compare with Tyneside and its people."
Hughie Gallacher

GATESHEAD Football Club longed to have the famous Hughie Gallacher in their ranks. The Redheugh Park side had made at least four attempts in previous years to bring the star back to Tyneside. There were some audacious moves, too, even trying to tempt the Scot to Third Division North football during his first season at Stamford Bridge, when a fee of £10,000 had just been paid, a huge amount that would have covered Gateshead's overheads for several years. None the less, they were ambitious and saw Gallacher, with his massive local following, as the answer perhaps to gaining elevation to Second Division and even First Division soccer. Additionally, Hughie's family had strong connections with the club. 'Tot' Anderson, his father-in-law, had been a Gateshead director for several years and George Mathison had recently left for Burnley after a good stint in Gateshead's defence.

On 8 June 1938, Gateshead eventually secured their man, for a mere £500. A year earlier, when he was still with Notts County, they had made a £1,000 offer, but now

Hughie, coming to the end of his career at Gateshead, pictured in the club's change strip of claret and blue.

only had to pay half that amount. Gateshead boss, secretary and chairman all in one, Bill Tulip, was more than pleased. Gallacher jumped at the move. A return to Tyneside where he had such a happy and fruitful five years — what could be better? Gateshead supplied a club house in Lobley Hill and Hughie said to an *Evening Chronicle* reporter: "It's grand to be back on Tyneside and my only regret is that I could not return two or three seasons ago; my heart has been here ever since I left United eight years ago." He added: "I have been north, south, east and the Midlands, but no place can compare with Tyneside and its people. My transfer to Gateshead is one of the greatest things that ever happened to me." He was to live out the rest of his life with his adopted folk in Gateshead.

Public interest in Tulip's scoop was astonishing and enthusiasm in the Gateshead club was rekindled, exactly, of course, what the shrewd Gateshead boss was hoping for. Trapped between giants Newcastle United and Sunderland, it had never been easy for the Redheugh side to enter the limelight. They had lived

constantly in the shadows of their illustrious neighbours. If it was not Newcastle who people talked about or watched, it was Sunderland, and rarely did Gateshead create the North-East's football news. The signing of Gallacher brought wild enthusiasm not only to the town of Gateshead but to Tyneside generally.

Gateshead, in fact, had a reasonable team. After having to seek re-election 12 months earlier, in 1937-8 they just missed promotion, ending the season in fifth place and scoring more goals than any other team in the bottom divisions. They always possessed ageing former stars, many of them ex-Sunderland and Newcastle players. Gallacher's teammates at St James' Park, Roddie McKenzie and Dave Davidson, had just completed spells there, while goalkeeper Albert McInroy was still at Redheugh Park. Gallacher was to give the side an

added boost — hopefully into the Second Division.

At the twilight of his career — he was now almost 36 — Hughie Gallacher still possessed charisma and could still perform his scintill-ating skills on the football pitch. Several, as usual, had doubts. Hughie had not been a success at Grimsby and many thought he was way past the point of retiring. One scribe also noted: 'And then there were the stories about him'. Could Gallacher keep out of trouble? Tulip had some doubts, too, but it was, in his opinion, worth the risk. Later into the season the Gateshead manager spoke of his earlier mis-givings: "Hughie? No bother, never misses training. The lads think the world of him — so do I. He brings them on a lot. Nothing is any trouble to him for the team."

Gallacher answered his critics in the only way he could, and as he had done in years gone by, with

goals. He bagged 18 in the season as he enjoyed what was to be his last fling, and he was kept out of controversy, too. His first game for his new club packed the fans in — 6,200 came along just to see Gateshead's pre-season trial game — while for the meeting with Newcastle United over 30,000 were attracted for the Football League Jubilee match. It turned out to be the second-highest attendance in the country as all clubs played local rivals in celebration of the League's 50th birthday. Only Tottenham's clash with Arsenal pulled in more than Gallacher's meeting with Newcastle. The Magpies won 2-1 and reports revealed: 'The Gallacher touches were there and Gateshead

Gallacher in discussion at Redheugh Park with Gateshead's Conroy (left) and Johns (right).

Rovers, then for the sixth occasion in his career he scored five goals in a match. Rotherham were on the receiving end of a 7-1 hiding. Gateshead's line-up on that September afternoon was:

Lawrence; Conroy, Livingstone, Heslop, Dudgeon, Cassidy, Thompson, Oxley, Gallacher, Embleton, Miller.

All eyes were on Rotherham's promising centre-forward, Walter Ardron. Many scouts were present at Redheugh but it was headline-stealer Gallacher they all watched. He put on a one-man show. The Gateshead goalkeeper for that game was Walter Lawrence. He recalled: "He scored some spectacular goals and was so very quick in thought. Rotherham's much younger players had no answer to Hughie's ball control and positioning. He was a class above everyone else."

people are now very keen to see him in a League game on their own ground'.

Hughie missed the opening Third Division North fixture at Crewe, being sent home on a train with influenza before the kick-off, but he made his League debut for the visit of Barrow on 31 August. He did not score in Gateshead's 2-1 win, but it was not long before Gallacher's size-six boots were sending the ball into the net once more. He was on the score-sheet against Doncaster

Hughie presenting medals and trophies at a local high-school sports day.

Gallacher was not only an added benefit to play alongside, but also good fun too. Lawrence said: "Hughie was a huge laugh. He had a great sense of humour and was an amazing character to be with in the dressing-room." Together with former England goalkeeper, Albert McInroy, who was another tremendous personality, it was laugh after laugh at Redheugh Park with frequent pranks and good-humoured banter. On the training pitch they had fun, with Gallacher acting as practical joker-in-chief. In between sprints he once gave goalkeeper Walter Lawrence a real fright, creeping up and pulling down his shorts when the Gateshead player was chatting to several girl fans on the terraces.

Crowds were up at Gateshead's Low Team ground, almost to the 20,000 mark, and expectation of a promotion challenge was high. Also to appear in Gateshead's black and white colours that season were locally-born half-backs George Neilson, who appeared over 250 times for the club, and Joe Inskip, ex-Sunderland. Billy Cassidy was

another prominent half-back and another born and bred on Tyneside, while up front, former Fulham winger Ed Miller and Bert Oxley had good seasons. Oxley grabbed ten goals alongside Gallacher and said of the centre-forward: "He was so good to play alongside, helping you all the time."

But fortunes dipped for the Tynesiders. In October, Gallacher missed several games through illness and results slumped. The Scot returned in December, but Gateshead had a tough job to secure the one promotion place. Gallacher inspired the team and they lost only two of the last 20 games. However, they finished a long way behind runaway champions, Barnsley. On 6 May 1939, Gateshead faced Carlisle United. The game ended in an unremarkable 1-1 draw, Gallacher hitting the net once more. It turned out to be the *coup de grâce* of his long career — Hughie's final goal in the top-class game in his last official match, although no one knew it at the time.

The rumblings and imminence of

A day on the beach for Gallacher and son.

1 August 1939. Pre-season training at Redheugh Park. Gallacher is in white shorts.

World War Two had been the focus of attention for many months and by the time footballers and fans should have been eagerly anticipating a new season, the crisis in Europe had reached its peak. The 1939-40 season kicked off on 26 August 1939, amidst an atmosphere of unreality. Gateshead lost 3-0 at Redheugh Park to Crewe Alexandra, while four days later they entertained Hartlepools in a local derby and won 3-0, Gallacher setting up two of the goals. On Friday, 1 September, Poland was invaded by Hitler's German forces, despite British Premier Chamberlain's warnings of the consequences. War loomed, but before the fateful day arrived, Gallacher played what was his last competitive match, albeit a Third Division fixture, later annulled from official records.

On Saturday, 2 September, he travelled with the Gateshead party to Lincoln and took part in an end-to-end match that finished in defeat for Gateshead by the odd goal in seven. Hughie did not close with a goal; he was well held by City's Askew. In fact he did not find the net in any of the three abortive matches, but he went close, netting with an offside 'goal' at Sincil Bank. Other newspaper stories that weekend concentrated on war preparations. Over 75,000 Newcastle and Gateshead children were evacuated from industrial Tyneside to the relative safety of the Northumberland and Durham countryside. King George VI made an emergency visit to 10 Downing Street to discuss events with the Prime Minister. Thousands of potential blood donors were being registered, while Parliamentary Bills were waiting to be rushed through the Commons, including the military call-up of all men between the ages of 18 and 41.

The following Sunday morning, at 11am, Chamberlain broadcast from the cabinet room of 10 Downing Street and announced that Britain was at war with Germany. The football season of 1939-40 was abandoned. Hughie Gallacher, like all professionals, had his contract cancelled. At 36 years of age, Gallacher's 20-year career in football came to a sudden end. It had been an extraordinary one and for two decades he was seldom missing from the centre of attraction and was always headline news. He was both adored and hated by differing factions of fans, while every conceivable accolade and rebuke was heaped upon him. There had been no more deadly centre-forward between the two world wars. He netted a formidable total of 463 goals in 624 senior games. Gallacher was the master opportunist and rip-roaring genius rolled into one. He could do things on the ball that simply couldn't be believed.

Raich Carter, England's talented inside-forward, rated him the greatest. He wrote in a newspaper column: 'There has never been

A family picture. Hughie and son, Hughie junior, then two and a half years old, pictured at their Gateshead home just before World War Two.

better', and added, 'His basic strong point was remarkable ball control. Because of it he had the ability to beat opponents in the minimum of space.' What made him that exquisite football genius was his great confidence — even to the point of being conceited and boastful — and his talent to perform the unexpected. He would turn up in the right place when it seemed impossible for him to get there and his feints, swerves and ability to go past players at ease, no matter how many, made him dangerous from any position. His shooting, perhaps, was his greatest gift. Gallacher possessed amazing strength in his short, stocky legs. He could poke a ball with immense power towards goal without taking much of a back swing. He would have a crack at goal with either foot, from all angles, even from the most acute and inconceivable of positions. For his minute size, 5ft 5in, he was deceivingly good in the air, too. Despite always being seemingly surrounded by giants, he had an amazing spring in his boots that sent him soaring above his opponent.

Hughie said of his own play: "Undoubtedly there were faster centre-forwards at the time, but I think I was the most skilful. I did not believe my job was solely to score goals, although naturally smacking the ball in the net was an important part." His awareness in and around the box was at times unreal. Dozens of chances came by way of a Gallacher deft flick, first-time pass or flash of dribbling skill. Hughie was able to bring the ball under control from any position or height, and he never allowed it to move far from his feet once in his power. His body remained well forward, shielding the ball and making it difficult for defenders to dispossess him.

Stamina and gritty determination are two ingredients that do not usually come with skilled ball players, but Gallacher had both. He was fearless and appeared to be able to run incessantly despite all the battering he received. Perhaps the non-stop chatter on the field and the constant teasing and insolence to opponents kept his mind involved in the game for the whole 90 minutes.

Now that was all over. Hughie Gallacher's career ended that Saturday afternoon at unglamorous Sincil Bank. The tenacious Scot had to start a new life without the constant roar of encouragement in his ears every match-day.

A fine portrait, as smart as ever.

CHAPTER FOURTEEN

TRAGIC FINALE

"People built him up as a hero figure — then they crucified him — as though he was a criminal."
Hughie Gallacher, junior

HUGHIE Gallacher could not keep off a football field for long. During the early days of the war he turned out for Gateshead in friendly matches against North-East opposition like Darlington, Middlesbrough and Newcastle United. But his days in these circles were limited. By 1940 he was playing local league football on Tyneside – no grand stadiums and no vast crowds. Now Gallacher graced the likes of Jarvis Park, Monkton, home of Bedewell Works FC in Hebburn, members of the Northern Combination and one of Hughie's teams during the hostilities.

Gallacher was losing his hair alarmingly now and sported a full short-back-and-sides, but he could still play a bit and was always willing to give encouragement. One goal-keeping colleague in those days remembered: 'He had a terrific volley, many times I've felt my chest shudder when I grabbed his shot. And he always came up to me, picked me off the ground and said, "Great save." '

Hughie worked in munitions factories which were commonplace along the Tyne. First in Gateshead

Gallacher during the war when serving as an ARP ambulance driver.

and then at Reyrolles Works in Jarrow, while he was also a member of the ARP — Air Raid Precautions — driving an ambulance based at Wrekenton in Gateshead. He was kept busy, too, as industrial Tyneside was a major target area and vulnerable to German air-raids from bases in Norway and Denmark. Those were days of gas-masks, black-outs, sirens and pronouncements of restraint, food and clothing rationing, coupons and evacuation. War affected everyone. Hughie's family was one of those evacuated. His son, Hughie junior, stayed in Lanarkshire with his grandparents for much of the war.

Gallacher also played exhibition matches in those war years to raise funds under the Wings for Victory banner. He was sometimes on the field for only 20 minutes but the crowd would always flock to see him. Also organized were ARP challenge games with Gallacher acting as manager and promoter, organizing and coaching from the sidelines as well as turning out for a half now and then. He took the job seriously, noting that any players he selected must be released from other duties for a complete week prior to the match. Games were fixed up with Newcastle United and Sunderland and other local sides. Hughie would proudly wear one of his Scotland jerseys when he took the select team for a training and coaching stint.

May 1945 saw the end of the war in Europe. Hughie Gallacher, now 42 years old, had to find a job like thousands of others. He quite fancied remaining in football and tried for a coaching position at both Gateshead and Newcastle. But neither offered him a job, despite the wealth of experience he could call upon. The former Scottish international tried over the border but could not get fixed up there either. Apparently his past explosive temperament went against him and also, as he had admitted to obtaining illegal payments, the FA would never consider him for a manager's post. Hughie gave up any aim of staying in the game and had to look elsewhere.

He craved to become a publican but his wife, Hannah, set her mind against that and Hughie found work on the Team Valley Industrial Estate in Gateshead, working as a non-skilled employee with several firms, including Patterson Lamps, De La Rue Printers, Taylor's Metal Workers and Huwoods. In the latter

The factory worker — overalls, protective gloves, yet still the neat shirt and tie.

factory he operated a shearing system producing machinery for Britain's coal-pits. He found new friends, chums that loved to talk football and to reminisce. He was now a working-class Tynesider with a soft Scots twang to his Geordie dialect. Gone were the white spats, tailored suits and bowler hat. Hughie now wore overalls and the traditional cloth cap, although he was always immaculately presented from head to foot.

For Hughie Gallacher the glory days were well and truly over. Yet he still kept his hand in the football scene and managed to get into bother with authority as usual. He covered local football as a personality journalist, tramping his way around grounds like Appleby Park, North Shields and Croft Park, Blyth, while he also wrote a regular column for the *Newcastle Evening Chronicle*. He often watched Newcastle United and Sunderland, the Roker team being surprisingly his favourite then, and was not afraid to criticize the North-East's

Gallacher the newspaper man with journalist Malcolm Usher (left) at the offices of the Newcastle Chronicle & Journal *in February 1952.*

big League outfits. The directors of Newcastle United did not like their past centre-forward's occasional harsh words and even withdrew ground passes to the Scot.

He was always on hand to give players advice at both St James' Park and Roker Park. Jackie Milburn recalled his meetings with Hughie: "Virtually every Saturday he'd be waiting for me outside the main entrance, always at the same place." Gallacher would give the United centre-forward many suggestions. "Hi, Jackie," he would say, "You're doing fine, but I've got a little tip for you, you're standing with your back to the centre-half and your teammates don't know how to play the ball up to you. Why don't you half turn to give them a clue which side you want it and then run. They'll never catch you." It was advice which Milburn took.

Gallacher the referee, in charge of a ladies match between Hazlerigg Womens Supporters Club and Dudley Ladies Physical Culture Club in September 1953.

The Celebrities v Harton Colliery Welfare at South Shields. Gallacher with son Hughie junior in centre is flanked on his left by Newcastle United's Joe Harvey.

A nostalgic return to Lanarkshire to play in an Airdrie Veterans match. Back row (left to right): McLay, Blake, McDonald, Stevenson, Paterson, Connor, Thomson. Front row: Watson, Suttie, Gallacher, Howieson, Mooney, Murray.

Gallacher wears the diamond jersey again, this time in aid of charity.

Hughie ran his local works team, Huwoods FC, and turned to refereeing as well. It was in this capacity that he was almost banned from football *sine die*. Gallacher had agreed to be in charge of a

charity game between unaffiliated clubs at Berwick, but the Durham Football Association, his local body, warned that if he refereed the game he could be contravening FA rules and could face an automatic ban from football. Hughie was furious. A charity game was a harmless event and again he considered that antiquated officials did not seem to be right. Gallacher ignored the FA warning and went ahead with his trip to the border town. Nothing happened at first, but a rift developed afterwards and some weeks later, senior FA official, Stanley Rous, met Gallacher to discuss his actions and agreed to sort matters out with the local FA.

What Hughie loved more than anything was to pull on his boots again. He appeared in charity games throughout the 1940s and 1950s — in veterans matches, which usually attracted crowds on Bank Holidays back in Scotland, or at the Horsley Hill ground at South Shields. He would never turn down an opportunity, saying to organizers: "All you have to do is lay on the transport, find some size-six boots and leave the rest to me."

One colleague recalled playing alongside Gallacher when he was 52 years of age and he scored a memorable goal even then. 'He took a cross from the wing, jammed it against the goalpost with his head and dropped it over the line — who else could do a thing like that?' Hughie played alongside local personalities like Jackie Milburn, Joe Harvey, Albert Stubbins, Charlie Ferguson and Warney Cresswell, while Alex James journeyed to Tyneside from London to help Gallacher's old-timers against a team of current professionals.

Hughie settled with his family in the Sheriff Hill area of Gateshead. He had three sons: Hughie Junior, Tommy and Matthew. All were born in Gallacher's footballing ports of call — Hughie Junior, the eldest, was born in Derby; Tommy in Nottingham; the youngest, Matthew, in Gateshead. Gallacher's oldest offspring followed his father's footsteps in football for a while, signing for Newcastle Juniors as a trialist in 1952. He scored on his debut but failed to make the grade at St James' Park, later having spells at Doncaster Rovers and Accrington Stanley.

Hughie Junior now resides on Tyneside while Tommy, known as 'Tot', lives in Anglesey after many tours of duty around the world with the RAF. Matthew emigrated in 1965 and now runs his own insurance company in Durban, South Africa. Gallacher also had family from his days in Bellshill. His son Jack, from his first marriage, went on to appear for Celtic from 1943 to 1950. He was good enough to be in the reckoning for Scotland's centre-forward spot in the wartime international against England in 1944, being understudy to Ephraim Dodds of Blackpool.

Hughie Gallacher's life was one with few mundane moments. Sensation, drama and incident followed him around. In 1950, when seemingly content with his out-of-football life, tragedy struck, not for the first or last time. On the very last day of the year, his wife Hannah died from a long standing heart complaint. Gallacher was shattered and his wife's sudden death affected him dramatically. He became depressed. Hannah's sister, Annie Mathison, recalled: "It reached him deeply. Hughie went downhill after

Jack Gallacher in Celtic colours c1945.

June 1950. Hughie senior and Hughie junior inspecting souvenirs.

the death and was never the same cheery individual again." His health was affected and physically his face became drawn. He slowly turned to frequenting pubs more and more, for company, and with it came drink.

Gallacher had always been branded as having a drink problem — unjustly so in his earlier days. Typical of the tales that circulated around Tyneside were his visits to the Half Moon in Gateshead, when he was still playing football. Gates-

head club skipper, Albert Watson, and goalkeeper, Walter Lawrence, would meet Hughie there for a quick drink before a home game. A half-pint later they would walk the short distance to Redheugh Park in time to change for the kick-off. Of course newspapers latched on to the story and blew the regular visits into a big sensation, with Gallacher in the headline; never did Watson or Lawrence get branded in the same way.

He now mixed with the hangers-on again, still evident and always wanting to talk football with a famous name. His big problem was

that he could not refuse their hospitality. Long-standing friend, George Mathison, said: "Hangers-on wouldn't leave him alone and he was not strong enough to ignore it." The former Newcastle and Gateshead footballer noted that drink changed his personality considerably and Gallacher himself said at one stage, "Drink has been my downfall."

Usually it started when Hughie would go out for a quiet drink with a pal. One such incident occurred on the way to watch Newcastle United. Gallacher and a friend called in to the Duke of York public house for a drink. He was spotted and a crowd gathered. Free drinks started to flow by the gallon and Hughie never made St James' Park that afternoon.

Hughie found that he had few real friends and with his elder sons away from home with the RAF, he had no one that he could turn to when he needed someone — and alcohol proved a false companion. It was with this background that the final, sad and dramatic, episode in Gallacher's life uncovered itself during the summer months of 1957.

In May of that year his son, Matthew, was removed from Hughie Gallacher's care by the local authority after complaints by the NSPCC. He was accused of assault, ill-treatment and neglect of his 14-year-old son after an incident in which Hughie lost his temper in a family dispute, threw an ashtray and caught his son on the side of the head. As usual with any incident involving the name of Hughie Gallacher, exaggerated stories quickly spread and he was handed a guilty judgement without trial. He was crucified by both media and street gossip. Gallacher idolized Matthew and the child's removal from his care literally broke his heart. Gallacher's eldest son, Hughie junior, said: "People built him up as a hero figure, one of the very best, then they crucified him when he was charged with assault, as though he was a criminal." The assault charge was an overstatement. Hughie junior continues: "Matti couldn't have done much wrong but caught

Gallacher wearing the Scotland cap from his last international, with son Matthew.

Hughie paying a visit to Redheugh Park, Gateshead, with his mother.

the quick temper of our father. He was cheeky, no doubt, and probably deserved scolding, an everyday occurrence today."

On Wednesday, 12 June 1957, Hughie Gallacher was summoned to appear before Gateshead Magistrates Court. But for Hughie, 12 June never came. By the previous day, his glittering career of almost 500 goals was far from his mind. He thought only of an unfortunate life — a broken early marriage, a deceased first child, a costly divorce,

the loss of his second wife, his loneliness and the prospect of facing a court with public and Press in full view on the most degrading of charges. It was an ordeal he could not face. He awoke that morning a worried and disturbed man. Instead of heading for work he went for a stroll, meeting a couple of relations and friends. They all later reported that he looked strange in manner. At midday, Hughie headed for the railway line at Low Fell station which ran near his home.

Down Belle Vue Bank he went, the road he walked every day to

work. Two train-spotters, one by coincidence the grandchild of one of Gallacher's ex-managers, Bill Tulip, saw him. The youngster said: "I noticed a small man wearing a cap, pacing up and down the footbridge. He kept looking up the line." Gallacher was intent on ending his life. He heard a train and stepped down from the bridge. Hughie climbed over the fence and knocked against one of the spotters. He said: "Sorry." Then he quickly walked up a cinder track. The train approached — the York-Newcastle-Edinburgh express — and as it thundered towards him, Hughie Gallacher jumped in front of it. He was killed instantly. The time was 12.08pm on 11 June 1957.

The decapitated body of the former goalscoring idol was found near the main line about 100 yards from a spot known locally as 'Dead Man's Crossing', a cruelly ironic title. He was 54 years old. That morning he had posted a letter to the Gateshead Coroner expressing regret at the trouble he had caused. He said that if he lived to be a hundred, he would never forgive himself for having struck Matthew. At the inquest the following Friday, the Coroner was told that Hughie had talked to a local journalist earlier in the week. He was reported to have said: "It's no good fighting this thing now. They have got me on this one. My life is finished. It is no use fighting when you know you can't win." The inquest returned a verdict of suicide.

Tributes were many and gratifying. The *Newcastle Journal's* headline was: 'Hughie of the Magic Feet is Dead'. The news of the manner of his death was a shock to all. Stan Seymour, so long a teammate, said: "I knew him more than 30 years and I say without hesitation that he was the greatest centre-forward I have ever seen. The ordinary rules didn't apply to Hughie Gallacher because he was a soccer genius." Another Newcastle personality, Jackie Milburn, said: "I literally wept the day I learned he had walked on to the railway crossing . . .how a man so loved and so idolized could feel so alone I'll never know." Charlie Buchan said, on hearing the news: "He was the complete leader of attack. I have seen faster and more thrustful leaders but none who combined the art of ball control, leadership and goalscoring as did Gallacher." Hughie's funeral was meant to be a private affair, but former teammates, club representatives and fans alike turned up, nevertheless, and lined the entrance to Newcastle Crematorium in their final appreciation.

Hughie Gallacher was a football immortal and in the opinion of many acknowledged judges of the game, the best centre-forward there has ever been. An immensely talented player — a natural if ever there was one — and a player who could never be copied, he was a one-off, born to football. His unpredictable and explosive temperament merely added to the fascination of the man and made him an even bigger box-office attraction. But no doubt in many ways he was a victim of his own fame.

His was a story that was inspiring, sometimes notorious, and tragic in its ending. Professional football has seen few greater, few more popular or more controversial players in its 104-year history. Without doubt Hughie Kilpatrick Gallacher is one of the true 'All Time Greats' of football, a legendary figure of the game.

Hughie pictured in his last years.

(bottom): Newcastle Evening Chronicle headlines . . . Tuesday 11 June 1957 and Friday 14 June 1957.

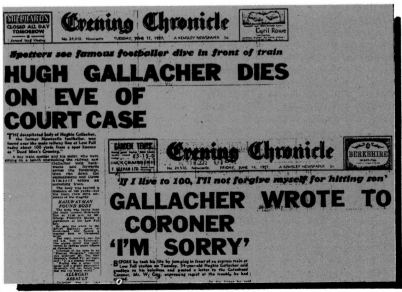

Appearances and Goals Summary
First-class football

Season	Club	League	League App	League Gls	Cup App	Cup Gls	Full caps App	Full caps Gls	Other int App	Other int Gls	TOTAL App	TOTAL Gls
1920-21	Queen of the South	Non-League			1	1					1	1
1921-22	Airdrieonians	Scottish League, Division 1	11	7	4	0					15	7
1922-23	Airdrieonians	Scottish League, Division 1	18	9	2	1					20	10
1923-24	Airdrieonians	Scottish League, Division 1	34	33	9	6	1	0			44	39
1924-25	Airdrieonians	Scottish League, Division 1	32	32	3	3	3	5	2	6	40	46
1925-26	Airdrieonians	Scottish League, Division 1	16	9			1	0	1	5	18	14
1925-26	Newcastle United	Football League, Division 1	19	23	3	2	2	3			24	28
1926-27	Newcastle United	Football League, Division 1	38	36	3	3	3	1			44	40
1927-28	Newcastle United	Football League, Division 1	32	21	1	0	2	1			35	22
1928-29	Newcastle United	Football League, Division 1	33	24	1	0	3	8			37	32
1929-30	Newcastle United	Football League, Division 1	38	29	6	5	3	6			47	40
1930-31	Chelsea	Football League, Division 1	30	14	1	0					31	14
1931-32	Chelsea	Football League, Division 1	36	24	5	6					41	30
1932-33	Chelsea	Football League, Division 1	36	19	1	0					37	19
1933-34	Chelsea	Football League, Division 1	23	13	5	3					29	16
1934-35	Chelsea	Football League, Division 1	7	2							7	2
1934-35	Derby County	Football League, Division 1	27	23	3	1	1	0	6	10	37	34
1935-36	Derby County	Football League, Division 1	24	15	1	1					25	16
1936-37	Notts County	Football League, Division 3 (S)	32	35	1	0					33	25
1937-38	Notts County	Football League, Division 3 (S)	13	7							13	7
1937-38	Grimsby Town	Football League, Division 1	12	3							12	3
1938-39	Gateshead	Football League, Division 3 (N)	31	18							31	18
1939-40	Gateshead	Football League, Division 3 (N)	3	0							3	0
			545	386	50	32	20	24	9	21	624	463

Club Totals

Queen of the South: 9 apps, 19 goals, a goal every 0.47 games (including non-League).
Airdrieonians: 129 apps, 100 goals, a goal every 1.29 games.
Newcastle United: 174 apps, 143 goals, a goal every 1.22 games.
Chelsea: 144 apps, 81 goals, a goal every 1.78 games.
Derby County: 55 apps, 40 goals, a goal every 1.38 games.
Notts County: 46 apps, 32 goals, a goal every 1.44 games.
Grimsby Town: 12 apps, 3 goals, a goal every 4 games.
Gateshead: 34 apps, 18 goals, a goal every 1.89 games.

Football League and FA Cup: 465 apps, 317 goals, a goal every 1.47 games.
Scottish League and Cup: 130 apps, 101 goals, a goal every 1.29 games.

Overall goals ratio: a goal every 1.35 games.

International Appearances

Scottish Full International Games

Date	Opponents	Venue	Score	Goals	Club
1 Mar 1924	Northern Ireland	Celtic Park	W 2-0		Airdrieonians
14 Feb 1925	Wales	Tynecastle	W 3-1	2	Airdrieonians
28 Feb 1925	Northern Ireland	Belfast	W 3-0	1	Airdrieonians
4 Apr 1925	England	Hampden Park	W 2-0	2	Airdrieonians
31 Oct 1925	Wales	Ninian Park	W 3-0		Airdrieonians
27 Feb 1926	Northern Ireland	Ibrox Park	W 4-0	3	Newcastle United
27 Apr 1926	England	Old Trafford	W 1-0		Newcastle United
30 Oct 1926	Wales	Ibrox Park	W 3-0	1	Newcastle United
26 Feb 1927	Northern Ireland	Belfast	W 2-0		Newcastle United
2 Apr 1927	England	Hampden Park	L 1-2		Newcastle United
29 Oct 1927	Wales	Wrexham	D 2-2	1	Newcastle United
31 Mar 1928	England	Wembley	W 5-1		Newcastle United
27 Oct 1928	Wales	Ibrox Park	W 4-2	3	Newcastle United
23 Feb 1929	Northern Ireland	Belfast	W 7-3	5	Newcastle United
13 Apr 1929	England	Hampden Park	W 1-0		Newcastle United
26 Oct 1929	Wales	Ninian Park	W 4-2	2	Newcastle United
22 Feb 1930	Northern Ireland	Celtic Park	W 3-1	2	Newcastle United
18 May 1930	France	Paris	W 2-0	2	Newcastle United
14 Apr 1934	England	Wembley	L 0-3		Chelsea
6 Apr 1935	England	Hampden Park	W 2-0		Derby County

Scottish League Games

Date	Opponents	Venue	Score	Goals	Club
14 Mar 1925	Football League	Goodison Park	L 3-4	1	Airdrieonians
11 Nov 1925	Irish League	Belfast	W 7-3	5	Airdrieonians

Scottish Tour of North America

Date	Opponents	Venue	Score	Goals	Club
18 May 1935	USA	Philadelphia	W 3-0	1	Derby County
22 May 1935	Ontario FA	Toronto	W 3-1	1	Derby County
29 May 1935	Alberta FA	Calgary	W 9-1	4	Derby County
1 Jun 1935	British Columbia	Vancouver	W 1-0	1	Derby County
5 Jun 1935	Manitoba FA	Winnipeg	W 7-2	2	Derby County
9 Jun 1935	USA	Newark	W 4-1	1	Derby County

International Summary

Scottish full international side	1924-35	20 games	24 goals
Scottish League side	1925	2 games	6 goals
Scottish Trial XI	1925	1 game	5 goals
Scottish Tour	1935	6 games	10 goals
Scottish Junior side	1920	1 game	1 goal
	Total	30 games	46 goals

- Gallacher's goals-per-game ratio is the best by any Scottish International.
- Gallacher was on the losing side in a Scotland match on only two occasions, both against England, in 1927 and 1934.
- Gallacher played at centre-forward in all his internationals.
- Gallacher registered four hat-tricks, or more goals, for Scotland.
- Gallacher is one of only three players to have scored the most goals in a Scottish League XI match, netting five against the Irish League in 1925.
- Gallacher is the only Scottish player to be credited with netting five goals in one international match, against Northern Ireland in 1929.

Club honours

Football League Championship:
...................1926-7 with Newcastle United.
Football League runners-up: 1935-6 with Derby County.
Scottish League runners-up:
.............1922-3, 1923-4, 1924-5 with Airdrieonians.
Scottish Cup winner: ....1924 with Airdrieonians.
FA Cup semi-finalist: ....1932 with Chelsea.

Thirty or more goals in a season

League and Cup games
39 ....for Newcastle United 1926-7 (a club record).
39...........................for Airdrieonians 1923-4.
35...........................for Airdrieonians 1924-5.
34 ....for Airdrieonians and Newcastle United 1925-6.
34 ....for Newcastle United 1929-30.
30 ....for Chelsea 1931-2.

Forty or more goals in a season

League, Cup and internationals
46 ....for Airdrieonians and Scotland 1924-5.
42 ...for Airdrie, Newcastle United and Scotland 1925-6.
40...........for Newcastle United and Scotland 1926-7.
40 ....for Newcastle United and Scotland 1929-30.

- For 12 successive years in the Football League, Gallacher was his club's top goalgetter.
- In 18 seasons in senior football, Gallacher topped his club's goal charts on no fewer than 15 occasions.

Five goals in a senior match

On six occasions
1st ....for Airdrieonians v Clyde, Division One at Broomfield Park, 29 Sep 1923.
2nd ....for Scotland B v Scotland, Trial Match at Tynecastle, 4 Mar 1925.
3rd...............for Scottish League v Irish League, at Belfast, 11 Nov 1925.
4th ....for Scotland v Ireland, at Belfast, 23 Feb 1929.
5th ....for Derby County v Blackburn Rovers, Division One at Ewood Park, 15 Dec 1934.
6th ....for Gateshead v Rotherham United, Division Three at Redheugh Park, 17 Sep 1938.

World ranking

Ratio of goals per game in international football
1 Ernst Willmonski Poland & Germany 43 gls/30 games
(1.43 goals/game)
2 Gunner Nordahl Sweden ....43 gls/33 games
(1.30 goals/game)
3 Hughie Gallacher Scotland ....24 gls/20 games
(1.20 goals/game)
4 Sven Rydell Sweden ....49 gls/43 games
(1.14 goals/game)
These figures are as Rothmans Yearbook 1983-4, which omits Steve Bloomer (28 gls/23 games — 1.21/game)

Scotland ranking

Goals in full international football
1 ......Kenny Dalglish ......30 goals in 102 games
2 ....Denis Law........30 goals in 55 games
3 .....Hughie Gallacher .....24 goals in 20 games
4 ....Lawrie Reilly ......22 goals in 38 games

League ranking

Goals in Scottish and English League football
1 ...Arthur Rowley ...1946-1965: 434 goals in 619 games
2 . Jimmy McGrory .1922-1938: 410 goals in 408 games
3 . Hughie Gallacher .1921-1939: 386 goals in 545 games
4 .....Dixie Dean.....1923-1937: 379 goals in 435 games

Aggregate transfer fees

A pre-war record
Airdrieonians to Newcastle United, 1925: £6,500
Newcastle United to Chelsea, 1930: £10,000
Chelsea to Derby County, 1934: £2,750
Derby County to Notts County, 1936: £2,000
Notts County to Grimsby Town, 1938: £1,000
Grimsby Town to Gateshead, 1938: £500
Aggregate: £22,750

H. GALLACHER

Gallacher's 'All-Time Greats' XI

As selected by Gallacher in the *Newcastle Evening Chronicle* 1950.

1
Elisha Scott
(Liverpool & Ireland);

2
Alex McNair
(Celtic & Scotland)

3
Ernie Blenkinsop
(Sheffield Wed & England)

4
Jimmy Gibson
(Villa & Scotland)

5
Jack Barker
(Derby County & England)

6
Jimmy McMullan
(Manchester City & Scotland)

7
Alec Jackson
(Chelsea & Scotland)

8
David Jack
(Arsenal & England)

9
Dixie Dean
(Everton & England)

10
Alex James
(Arsenal & Scotland)

11
Alan Morton
(Rangers & Scotland)

Milestones

February 1903 ....Born Bellshill, Lanarkshire
March 1920..Joined Bellshill Athletic
July 1920 ....Married to Annie McIlvaney
December 1920...Selected for Scotland Junior XI
December 1920 ....Signed for Queen of the South
May 1921...Transferred to Airdrieonians
September 1921 ....Scottish League debut v Raith Rovers
March 1924.......................................First Scottish cap v Northern Ireland
April 1924 ....Scottish Cup victory over Hibernians
November 1925 ....Netted five goals for Scottish League
December 1925......................Newcastle United paid a record £6,500 transfer
December 1925.....................Football League debut v Everton, scoring twice
April 1927 ....Skippered the Magpies to League Championship
January 1928..Suspended for two months by FA
March 1928..................Took part in the Wembley Wizards match at Wembley
February 1929 ....Scored five goals for Scotland v Northern Ireland
May 1930..Chelsea paid £10,000 for his talents
September 1930 ....Record crowd saw his return to Newcastle
January 1931.................................Suspended again for almost two months
March 1932 ....Reached FA Cup semi-final with Chelsea
March 1934 ....Suspended once more by the FA
September 1934 ....Married to Hannah Anderson
October 1934 ....Appeared in bankruptcy court
November 1934....................................Signed by Derby County for £2,750
April 1935 ....Last full game for Scotland
May 1936.............................Runners-up in Division One with Derby County
September 1936...............................Transferred to Notts County for £2,000
January 1938...............................Grimsby Town paid £1,000 for his services
June 1938 ....A return to Tyneside with Gateshead for £500
September 1939........................Last League match before war halted football
June 1957 ....Demise at 'Dead Mans Crossing' Gateshead

Bibliography

Books etc.
Brodie, M., *100 Years of Irish Football*.
Busby, M., *My Story*.
Cheshire, S. & Hockings, R., *Chelsea: Full Statistical Story*.
Cormack, I.L., *Old Bellshill*.
Crampsey, R., *The Scottish Footballer*.
Docherty-Thomson, *100 Years of Hibs*.
Ekberg, C. & Woodhead, S., *The Mariners (History of Grimsby Town)*.
Esther, G., *Requiem for Redheugh (History of Gateshead)*.
Finn, R., *A History of Chelsea*.
Gibson, J., *The Newcastle United Story*.
Harding, J., *Alex James: Life of a Football Legend*.
James, B., *England v Scotland*.
Jardine, W., *The Queens 1919-1969 (History of Queen of the South)*.
Joannou, P., *Newcastle United: A Complete Record 1882-1986*.
Joannou, P., *A Complete Who's Who of Newcastle United*.
Joannou, P., *The History of Newcastle United*.
Keevans, H. & McCarra, K., *100 Cups (History of Scottish Cup)*.
Lamming, D., *A Scottish Soccer International Who's Who*.
Lamming, D., *A Who's Who of Grimsby Town*.
McCarra, K., *Scottish Football*.
McGlone, D. & McClure, W., *The Juniors, 100 Years*.
McPhail, R. & Harron, A., *Legend*.
Mackay, J.R., *The Hibees (History of Hibernian)*.
Milburn, J., *Jackie Milburn's Newcastle United Scrapbook*.
Mortimer, J.G., *Derby County: A Complete Record 1884-1988*.
Rafferty, J., *100 Years of Scottish Football*.
Rippon, A., *Eng-land! The Story of the National Soccer Team*.
Rippon, A. & Ward A., *The Derby County Story*.
Robertson, F.H.C., *The New Scottish Football Factbook*.
Ward, A., *Scotland The Team*.
Warsop, K. *The Magpies (History of Notts County)*.

Annuals & Magazines
AFS Annuals — various editions
Athletic News Annuals — 1919-1939.
The County of Lanark, 3rd Statistical Account 1960.
Gamages Annuals — 1919-1929.
Northern Echo Annuals — 1926-1939.
Rothmans Football Yearbooks — 1970-1989.
Scottish Football Historian magazine — various editions.
Scottish Football Association minutes — 1934-1936.

Newspapers
The Coatbridge Express — 1921 to 1925.
Dumfries & Galloway Standard — 1921.
Daily Record — 1921 to 1925.
Newcastle Daily Chronicle — 1925 to 1957.
Newcastle Daily Journal — 1925 to 1936.
Derby Evening Telegraph — 1935 to 1936.
South Shields Gazette — 1925 to 1930.

Specific Articles
Franks, D., *The Genius in Size-6 Boots*, Daily Mail, 1961.
Gallacher, H., *Ups and Downs of My Football Life*, Sunday Post, 1931.
North East's 100 Greatest Footballers, Newcastle Journal, 1972.
Hughie Gallacher Tells All, Newcastle Weekly Chronicle, 1950.
Kirkup, Dick, *The Hughie Gallacher Story*, 1974.

Other titles available from
Breedon Books

Title	Price	ISBN No.
Grimsby Town: A Complete Record 1878-1989	£14.95	0 097969 46 1
Plymouth Argyle: A Complete Record 1903-1989	£14.95	0 097969 40 2
Hull City: A Complete Record 1904-1989	£14.95	0 097969 49 6
Birmingham City: A Complete Record 1875-1989	£14.95	0 097969 48 8
Bolton Wanderers: A Complete Record 1877-1989	£14.95	0 097969 51 8
Oxford United: A Complete Record 1893-1989	£14.95	0 097969 52 6
Leeds United: A Complete Record 1919-1989	£14.95	0 097969 50 X
Middlesbrough: A Complete Record 1876-1989	£14.95	0 097969 53 4
Crystal Palace: A Complete Record 1905-1989	£14.95	0 097969 54 2
NASL: Record of the N.American Soccer League	£17.95	0 097969 56 9
Hartlepool United: A History	£9.95	0 097969 57 7
Who's Who of Liverpool FC 1892-1989	£4.95	0 097969 55 0
Spurs: A Complete Record 1882-1988	£14.95	0 097969 42 9
Bradford City: A Complete Record 1903-1988	£14.95	0 097969 38 0
Oldham Athletic: A Complete Record 1907-1988	£14.95	0 097969 36 4
Derby County: A Complete Record 1884-1988	£14.95	0 097969 39 9
Arsenal: A Complete Record 1886-1988	£14.95	0 097969 41 0
Everton: A Complete Record 1879-1988	£14.95	0 097969 43 7
Liverpool: A Complete Record 1892-1988	£14.95	0 097969 44 5
West Ham United: A Complete Record 1900-1987	£14.95	0 097969 29 1
Fulham: A Complete Record 1879-1987	£14.95	0 097969 28 3
Sheffield Wednesday: A Complete Record 1867-1987	£14.95	0 097969 25 9
Manchester City: A Complete Record 1887-1987	£14.95	0 097969 24 0
Saints: A Complete Record 1885-1987	£14.95	0 097969 22 4
Albion: A Complete Record 1879-1987	£14.95	0 097969 23 2
Aberdeen: A Complete Record 1903-1987	£14.95	0 097969 30 5
Aston Villa: A Complete Record 1874-1988	£14.95	0 097969 37 2
Scotland The Team	£9.95	0 097969 34 8
Funny Game, Football	£2.95	0 097969 21 6
Pompey's Gentleman Jim	£9.95	0 097969 45 3
The Illustrated Footballer	£6.95	0 097969 47 X

Breedon Books Publishing Co.
44 Friar Gate, Derby DE1 1DA.